ACCLAIM FOR *BURNED ALIVE*

"Riveting."

—*Reader's Digest* (Editors' Choice)

★ ★ ★

"Chillingly parallel to Margaret Atwood's *The Handmaid's Tale* . . . Designed to enrage and inform, and it does so with relentless energy."
—*Cleveland Plain Dealer*

★ ★ ★

"This memoir, although painful to read, will be of urgent interest to anyone concerned with international human rights."
—*Publishers Weekly*

★ ★ ★

"A rare artifact."

—*Washington Post Book World*

★ ★ ★

"An important book."

—*Milwaukee Journal Sentinel*

Burned Alive

A Survivor of an "Honor Killing" Speaks Out

———

SOUAD

In Collaboration with

MARIE-THERESE CUNY

GRAND CENTRAL
PUBLISHING

NEW YORK   BOSTON

Grand Central Publishing
Hachette Book Group
237 Park Avenue
New York, NY 10017

www.HachetteBookGroup.com

Printed in the United States of America
Published in hardcover by Hachette Book Group.
First U.S. Trade Edition: May 2005
10 9 8 7 6 5

Grand Central Publishing is a division of Hachette Book Group, Inc.
The Grand Central Publishing name and logo is a trademark of Hachette Book Group,
Inc.

The Library of Congress has cataloged the hardcover eition as follows:

Souad.
    Burned alive : a victim of the law of men / Souad.
        p. cm.
    ISBN 0-446-53346-7
    1. Honor killings—Palestine—Case studies. 2. Abused women—Palestine—Biography.
3. Souad. I. Title.
    HV6197.P19S68 2004
    362.82'92'092—dc22

2003027194

ISBN: 978-0-446-69487-2 (pbk.)

Book design by Giorgetta Bell McRee
Cover photo by Jean Marie Perier/At Large

Contents

Burned Alive

I Was in Flames

I am a girl. A girl must walk fast, head down, as if counting the number of steps she's taking. She may never stray from her path or look up, for if a man were to catch her eye, the whole village would label her a *charmuta*. If a married neighbor woman, or an old woman, or just anybody were to see her out without her mother or her older sister, without her sheep, her bundle of hay, or her load of figs, they would right away say *charmuta*. A girl must be married before she can raise her eyes and look straight ahead, or go into a shop, or pluck her eyebrows and wear jewelry. My mother was married at fourteen. If a girl is still unmarried by that age, the village begins to make fun of her. But a girl must wait her turn in the family to be married. The oldest daughter first, then the others.

There are too many girls in my father's house, four of marrying age. There are also two half sisters, born of our father's second wife, who are still children. The one male child of the family, the son who is adored by all, is our brother Assad, who was born in glory among all these daughters. He is the fourth born. I am the third.

Adnan, my father, is not happy with my mother, Leila, for giving him all these girls. He is unhappy, too, with his other wife,

Aicha, who also has given him nothing but girls. Noura, the oldest daughter, was married late when I myself was about fifteen. Nobody has yet asked for Kainat, the second girl, who is about a year older than me. I did overhear that a man spoke to my father about me, but he was told that I must wait for Kainat's marriage before I can marry. But Kainat may not be pretty enough, and is probably too slow at her work. I'm not really sure why she hasn't been asked for, but if she stays unmarried, she'll be the butt of the village jokes, and so will I.

It is a curse in my village to be born a girl. I have no memory of having played games or having fun as a child. The only freedom a girl can dream about is marriage, leaving your father's house for your husband's and not coming back, even if you're beaten. It is considered shameful for a married daughter to return home because she is not supposed to ask for protection outside her husband's house. If she does return to her father's house, it is her family's duty to bring her back to her husband. My sister was beaten by her husband and she brought shame on our family when she came back home to complain.

She is lucky to have a husband, though. I dream about it. Ever since I heard that a man spoke to my father about me, I have been consumed by impatience and curiosity. I know he lives three or four steps from us. Sometimes I can catch sight of him from the upper terrace where I lay the laundry out to dry. He must have a good job in the city because he never dresses like a laborer. He always wears a suit, carries a briefcase, and has a car. I'd like to see his face close up but I'm afraid the family will catch me spying. So when I go to get hay for a sick sheep in the stable, I walk fast hoping to see him nearby. But he parks his car too far away. From watching, I know about what time he comes out to go to work. So at seven o'clock in the morning, I pretend to be folding the laundry on the terrace or looking for a ripe fig or shaking out the carpets to get a glimpse of him driving off in his car. I have to be quick so I won't be noticed. What I do is climb the stairs and pass through the rooms to get to the terrace. There I energetically shake a rug and look over the cement wall, just slightly glancing to the right. If somebody notices me from afar, they won't guess that I'm looking down at the street.

When I see him, I realize I am in love with this man and this car! I imagine many things on the terrace: I am married to him and, like today, I watch the car go off into the distance until I can't see it anymore. But he'll come back from work at sunset and I will remove his shoes, and on my knees I will wash his feet as my mother does for my father. I will bring him his tea, and I'll watch him smoke his long pipe, seated like a king in front of the door of his house. I will be a woman who has a husband!

And maybe I'll even be able to put on makeup, get into this car with my husband, and even go into town and into the shops. I will endure the worst for the simple freedom of being able to go through this doorway to go out and buy bread! But I will not ever be a *charmuta*. I will not look at other men. I will continue to walk fast, erect and proud, but will not watch my steps with lowered eyes, and the village will not be able to say bad things about me, because I will be a married woman.

It is from this very terrace that my terrible story began. I was already older than my older sister was on the day of her wedding. I must have been eighteen, or maybe more, I don't know, and I both hoped and I despaired. My memory went up in smoke the day the flames engulfed me, but I have tried to reconstruct what happened.

Memory

I was born in a tiny village that, I'm told, was somewhere in the West Bank. But since I never went to school, I don't know anything about my country's history. I have also been told that I was born there in either 1957 or 1958, so I'm about forty-five years old today. Twenty-five years ago, I spoke only Arabic; I'd never been farther than a few kilometers beyond the last house on the dirt road. I knew there were cities farther away but I never saw them. I did not know if the earth was round or flat, and I had no idea of the world in general. What I did know was that we had to hate the Jews who had taken our land; my father called them pigs. We were forbidden to go near them, to speak or come in contact with them for fear of becoming a pig like them.

I had to say my prayers at least twice a day. I recited them like my mother and sisters, but I only learned of the Koran in Europe many years later. My only brother, treated like the king of the house, went to school, but the girls did not. As I've mentioned, where I come from, being born a girl was a curse. A wife must first produce a son, at least one, and if she gives birth to only girls, she is mocked. Two or three girls at most are needed for the house-work, to work on the land, and see to the animals. If more girls are born, it is a great misfortune and they should be gotten rid of as soon as possible. I lived this way until about the age of seventeen without knowing anything except that I was valued less than an animal because I was a girl.

So, this was my first life, as an Arab woman in the West Bank. It lasted twenty years, and the person I had been there died. She is no more.

My second life began in Europe at the end of the 1970s in an international airport. I was not much more than suffering human flesh on a stretcher. My body smelled so much of death that the passengers on the plane that was taking me from Palestine to Europe protested. Even though I was hidden behind a curtain, my presence was unbearable to them. As I write about it now, I relive that moment: They tell me that I am going to live but I do not believe that and I wait for death. I even beg for it to take me. Death seems preferable to this suffering and humiliation. There is almost nothing left of my body so why would they want to keep me alive when I don't wish to exist anymore, either my body or my mind?

I still think about that today. It is true that I would have preferred to die rather than face this second life that they were so generously offering me. But, in my case, to have survived is a miracle. It allows me now to bear witness in the name of all those women who have not had this opportunity, and who keep dying for this one reason, that they are women.

I had to learn French by listening to people speak and by forcing myself to repeat the words they explained to me with signs: "Bad? Not bad? Eat? Sleep? Walk?" I answered by making signs of yes or no. Much later I learned to read words in a newspaper, patiently day after day. In the beginning I could only decipher short announcements, death notices, or brief sentences with a few words that I would repeat phonetically. Sometimes I felt like an animal that was being taught to communicate as a human. In my head, in Arabic, I asked myself where I was, in what country, and why I hadn't died in my village. I was ashamed to be still alive, although no one knew this. I was afraid of this life but no one understood.

I have to say all this before attempting to reassemble the pieces of my memory, because I want these words to be inscribed in a book.

I remember very little of my earliest childhood, and my memory is still full of gaps. The first part of my life is made up of images that are strange and violent, like scenes in a film for television. I have so much difficulty putting these images back in order that it sometimes doesn't seem real. For example, how could I forget the name of one of my sisters, or my brother's age the day of his wedding, but yet remember everything about the goats, the lambs, the cows, the bread oven, the laundry in the garden, picking the cauliflowers, the squash, the tomatoes and figs . . . the stable and the kitchen . . . the sacks of wheat and the snakes? Or the terrace where I spied on my beloved? The wheat field where I committed the "sin"?

Sometimes a color or an object strikes me, and then an image will come back to me, maybe a person, or voices, or faces that all blend together. Often when I'm asked a question, my mind goes completely blank. I desperately look for an answer and it won't come. Or another image suddenly comes to me and I don't know what it corresponds to. But these images are imprinted in my head and I will never forget them. After all, you can't forget your own death!

My name is Souad. I am from the West Bank. As a child, with my sister, I look after the sheep and the goats because my father has a flock of goats, and I work harder than a beast of burden. I must have started to work at about age eight or nine, and I saw the blood of my first menstrual period at about ten. Among us, they say a girl is mature or "ripe" when this occurs. I was ashamed of this blood because I had to hide it, even from my mother's eyes, and wash my pants secretly to make them white again, and then dry them quickly in the sun so the men and the neighbors wouldn't see them. Two pairs were all I had. I remember the paper I used for protection on these awful days when you are considered to have the plague. I would bury it, the sign of my impurity, in secret in the garbage pail. If I had cramps, my mother would boil sage leaves and give it to me to drink. She wrapped my head tightly in a scarf and the next day I had no more pain. It is the only medicine I remember and I still use it because it works.

In the early mornings I go to the stable, where I whistle using my fingers for the sheep to gather around me, and then leave for the pasture with my sister Kainat, the one who is about a year older than me. Girls are not to go out alone but should be accompanied by someone older. The elder serves as safeguard for the younger. My sister Kainat is nice, round and a little chubby, while I am small and thin. We get along well. The two of us would go with the sheep and the goats to the field, about a quarter of an hour's walk from the village, walking fast and with eyes lowered as far as the last house. Once we were in the field, we were free to say silly things to each other and even laugh a little, but I don't remember any real conversation between us. Mostly, we ate our cheese, feasted on a watermelon, and watched the sheep and especially the goats, which were capable of devouring all the leaves of a fig tree in a few minutes. When the sheep moved into a circle to sleep, we fell asleep in the shade, risking having an animal wander into a neighboring field, and suffering the consequences when we got home. If an animal tore up a vegetable garden or if we were a few minutes late getting back to the stable, we got a thrashing with a belt.

Our village is very pretty and green. There are many fruits, such as figs, grapes, lemons, and an enormous number of olive trees. My father owns half the cultivated parcels of the village, all his. He isn't very rich but he has possessions. Our stone house is big, and is surrounded by a wall with a large door of gray iron. This door is the symbol of our captivity. Once we're inside, it closes on us to prevent us from going out. You can enter by this door from the outside, but you cannot go out again.

Is there a key or is it an automatic system? I remember my father and mother going out, but not us. My brother, on the other hand, is as free as the wind. He goes to the movies; he goes out and he comes back through this door, doing whatever he wants. I would often look at it, this awful iron door, and say to myself, *I'll never be able to leave through there, never . . .*

I don't have a good sense of the village because I'm not able to go out when and where I please. If I close my eyes and make an effort, I can tell what I've seen of it. There is my parents' house, then the one I call the rich people's house a little farther on the same side. Opposite is the house of my beloved, which I can see from the terrace. You cross the road and there it is. There are also a few other scattered houses, but I don't know how many—very few anyway. They are surrounded by low walls or iron fences and the people have vegetable gardens like us. I've never been through the entire length of the village. I only leave the house to go to market with my father and my mother or to the fields with my sister and the sheep. That's all.

Until I was seventeen or eighteen, I had seen nothing else. I had not set foot a single time in the shop in the village near the house, but in passing by in my father's van to go to market, I would always see the merchant standing at his door smoking his cigarettes. The shop has separate entrances for men and women. The men use the one on the right to go in and buy their cigarettes, newspapers, and drinks, and on the left are the fruits and vegetables where the women shop. In another house on the same side of the road as our house lives a married woman with four children. She has the right to go out and she can go into the shop. I see her standing on the stairs of the fruit-and-vegetable side holding transparent plastic sacks.

There was a lot of land around our house that was full of vegetables we had planted: squash, cauliflower, and tomatoes. Our garden was separated from the garden of the neighboring house by a low wall that was possible to step over, although none of us ever did. Being closed in was normal. It would never have occurred to any of the girls of the house to cross this symbolic barrier. To go where? Once in the village or on the road, a girl all alone would very quickly be spotted and her reputation and the family's honor would be destroyed.

It was inside this garden that I did the laundry. There was a well in one corner, and I heated the water in a basin over a wood fire. I would take a bundle of kindling from the supply and would break the branches over my knee. It took some time to heat the water but I did other things while I waited. I swept, washed the ground, and saw to the vegetables in the garden. Then I did the laundry by hand and would lay it out on the terrace to dry in the sun.

The house was modern and very comfortable, but for many years we had no hot water in the bathroom or the kitchen. It had to be heated outside and carried in. Later on, my father had hot water installed and brought in a bathtub and shower. All the girls used the same water for washing, but my brother had the right to his own water, and certainly my father also.

At night I slept with my sisters on the ground on a sheepskin. When it was very hot we slept on the terraces, lined up under the moon. We girls were next to each other in a corner. My parents and my brother slept in another part.

The workday began early. At sunrise if not earlier, my father and mother would get up. When it was the time for harvesting the wheat, we would bring something to eat with us and everybody worked, my father, my mother, my sisters, and me, but not my brother. When it was time to gather the figs, we would also set out very early because they had to be picked one by one, without missing a single one. We put them into crates and my father would take them to market. It was a good half hour's walk with the donkey to a small town, really very small, and whose name I've forgotten, if I ever knew it. Half of the market at the town's entrance was reserved for produce and the merchants who were there to sell it. To shop for clothes, you had to take the bus to a larger town. But we girls never went there. My mother would go with my father. It was like this: She'd buy a dress with my father and then she'd give it to one of us. Whether you like it or not, you have to

11

wear it. Neither my sisters nor I, nor even my mother, had anything to say about it. It was that dress or nothing.

Girls wore long dresses with short sleeves made of a type of cotton, a very warm material that pricked your skin. They were gray or sometimes white, or very rarely black. The collar was high and tightly fastened. Over this we had to put a long-sleeved shirt or a vest, according to the season. It was sometimes so hot that it was stifling, but long sleeves were required. To show a bit of arm or leg—or worse, any skin below the neck—brought shame. Under the long dress we wore the *saroual*, which are long baggy pants that are gray or white. Worn beneath these was a pair of underpants that were cut big like shorts and that reached above the stomach. All my sisters dressed like this, too. Women usually did not wear shoes, except sometimes married women, so we were barefoot all the time.

My mother was often dressed in black. My father wore a white *saroual*, plus a long shirt and the traditional red-and-white head scarf. My father! I can see him sitting under a tree on the ground in front of our house, his cane nearby. He is small and has a pale complexion with red splotches, a round head, and very mean blue eyes. One day he broke his leg in a fall from a horse and we girls were so pleased because it meant that he couldn't run after us as fast as before to beat us with his belt.

I see him very clearly, our father. I can never forget him. It is as if I carry a photograph of him in my head. He is sitting in front of his house like a king before his palace, with his red-and-white scarf that covers his bald red skull, he's wearing his belt and his cane rests on the leg folded under him. He is small and mean. He takes off his belt and he shouts: "Why have the sheep come back by themselves?"

He pulls me by the hair and he drags me on the ground into the kitchen. He strikes me while I kneel, he pulls on my braid as if he wants to pull it out, and he cuts it off with the big scissors used for shearing wool. I have hardly any hair left. I can cry, yell, or plead but I'll get only more kicks.

It really is my fault about the sheep. I had fallen asleep with my sister because it was so hot, and I let the sheep go off on their own. He hits so hard with his cane that sometimes I can't lie down on either my left or my right side because I am in so much pain. With the belt or the cane, I think we were beaten every day. A day without a beating was unusual.

I think maybe it was this time that he tied us up, Kainat and me, our hands behind our backs, our legs bound, and a scarf over our mouths to keep us from screaming. We stayed like that all night, tied to a gate in the big stable. We were with the animals, but were worse off than they were.

This is what it was like in our village. It was the law of men. The girls and the women were certainly beaten every day in the other houses, too. You could hear the crying. It was not unusual to be beaten, to have your hair shaved off and be tied to a stable gate. There was no other way of living.

My father, the all-powerful man, the king of the household, who owns, who decides, who strikes and tortures us! And he sits there calmly smoking his pipe in front of his house with his women, whom he treats worse than his livestock, locked up. A man takes a woman in order to have sons, to have her serve him as a slave like the daughters who will come, if she has the misfortune to produce any.

I often thought when I looked at my brother, who was adored by the whole family including me: *What more does he have? What makes him so special? He came out of the same belly as I did.* And I had no answer. That was just the way it was. We girls had to serve him as we did my father, groveling and with head lowered. I can also picture the tea tray. You had to bring even this tea tray to the men of the family with your head down, looking only at your feet, with back bent, and in silence. You don't speak. You only speak in answer to a question.

At noon, it's sugared rice, vegetables with chicken or mutton, and always bread. In my father's house, the garden gives us almost everything we need for food. And we do everything ourselves. My father buys only sugar, salt, and tea. There is always food to eat; the family lacks nothing for meals. In the morning I make tea for the girls, I pour a little olive oil onto a plate, with olives on the side, and I heat the water in a basin on the coals of the bread oven. The dried green tea is in a sack of tan cloth on the floor in a corner of the kitchen. I plunge my hand into the sack, I take a handful and put it into the teapot, I add sugar, and I return to the garden for the hot basin. It's heavy and I have trouble carrying it by its two handles, my back arched, so as not to burn myself. I come back into the kitchen and I pour the water into the teapot, slowly, over the tea and the sugar. I know that if I drop any on the floor, I'll be beaten. So I pay attention. If I'm clumsy, I shouldn't sweep it up, but rather collect it and put it back in the teapot. Then my sisters come to eat, but my father, mother, and brother are never with us. In this picture of tea drunk in the morning, sitting on the floor in the kitchen, I always see only sisters. I try to situate my age but it's difficult. I do know that the eldest, Noura, isn't married yet.

As for outside work, there is a lot of fruit. Grapes grow along the terrace, where I pick them. There are oranges, bananas, and mainly the black and green figs. And a memory that I'll never lose is of going out early in the mornings to pick the figs. They have opened a little with the evening coolness and they run like honey, the purest of sweets.

The sheep are the really heavy work. Take them out, lead them to the fields, watch over them, bring them back, cut the wool that my father is going to take to the market to sell. I take a sheep by its hooves and get it to lie down on the ground so I can tie it up and I clip the wool with the big shears. They are so big for my small hands that I have trouble using my hands after only a few minutes. And I milk the ewes while sitting on the ground. I squeeze their hooves between my legs and I pull the milk, which is used to make cheese. When the milk cools off you drink it just like that, fat and nourishing.

In general, I am incapable of organizing my memories by my age at the time, but I think my memory is about right, give or take one or two years. I am more certain of events around the time of Noura's marriage when I was about fifteen.

My sister Kainat is still at home, older by a year and not married. And then there is another sister after me whose name escapes me. I try to remember her name, but it doesn't come to me. I have to call her something in order to talk about her, so I'll call her Hanan, but may she forgive me because it surely isn't her name. I know she took care of the two little half sisters my father brought home after he abandoned his second wife, Aicha. I have seen this woman and I did not have ill feelings toward her. It was considered acceptable for my father to have taken her. He always wanted to have sons, but it didn't work out with Aicha, either. She gave him only two more girls, still more girls! So he dropped her and brought the two new little sisters home. That was considered the normal thing to do. Everything the men wanted to do was considered normal in this village, including my father's striking us with the cane, and all the rest. I couldn't imagine any other kind of life. Besides, I didn't really imagine anything at all. There were no precise thoughts in my head. In our childhood, we knew no play or toys, no games, only obedience and submission.

In any case, these two little girls live with us now and Hanan stays at home to take care of them, of that I'm sure. But their names, too, are unhappily forgotten. I just refer to them as "the little sisters." In my first memories of them, they are about five or six years old and they don't work yet. They are in Hanan's care and she very rarely leaves the house, except when it is necessary for picking vegetables in season.

In our family, the children are about a year apart. My mother was married at fourteen, my father much older than her. She has had many children, fourteen in all, she says. Only five are still living. For a long time I didn't realize what giving birth to fourteen children meant. One day my mother's father was talking about it while I served the tea. I can still hear his words in my ears: "It's good that you married young, you were able to have fourteen children . . . and a son, it's very good."

Even if I didn't go to school, I knew how to count the sheep. So I could count on my hands that there were only five of us, Noura, Kainat, me Souad, Assad, and Hanan, not fourteen. Where were the others? My mother never said that they had died but it was acknowledged in her usual comment: "I have fourteen children, seven of them are living." She included the half sisters with us five, since we never said "half sisters," always "sisters." It would seem that there were then seven others missing. But really nine were missing, if the half sisters weren't counted. Either way, many of the children she had borne were not still alive.

But one day I learned why there were only seven of us in the house. I can't say how old I was, but I wasn't yet at puberty, so I was less than ten years old. Noura the oldest is with me. I have forgotten many things, but not what I saw with my own eyes, terrorized, but not really aware that it was a crime.

I see my mother lying on the floor on a sheepskin. She is giving birth, and my aunt Salima is with her sitting on a cushion. There are cries from my mother and then from the baby, and very quickly my mother takes the sheepskin and she smothers the baby. She is on her knees. I see the baby move under the blanket and then it's over. I don't remember what happened after that, I just know that the baby isn't there anymore. That's all, and a terrible fear grips me.

So it was a girl that my mother suffocated at her birth. I saw her do it this first time, then a second time. I'm not sure I was present for the third one, but I knew about it. And I hear my sister Noura say to my mother: "If I have girls, I'll do what you have done."

This is how my mother got rid of the seven girls that she had after Hanan, the last survivor. This was accepted as normal. I accepted it, too, but I was also terrified. These little girls my mother was killing were a little of me. I started to hide and cry every time my father would kill a sheep or a chicken, because I was trembling for my life. The death of an animal, like that of a baby, was so simple and so ordinary a thing for my parents, but it set off in me a fear of disappearing as simply and as quickly as these babies had. I would tell myself that it's going to be my turn one of these days, or my sister's. They can kill us whenever they want. Big or small, there's no difference. Since they've given us life, they have the right to take it.

As long as you live with your parents in my village, the fear of death is there. I'm afraid of going up on a ladder when my father is down below. I'm afraid of the hatchet that is used for chopping the wood, afraid of the well when I go for water. Afraid when my father watches the sheep returning to the stable with us. Afraid of the noise of a door at night, of being suffocated in the sheepskin that is my bed.

Sometimes, coming back from the fields with the animals, Kainat and I talk about it a little: "And supposing everybody's dead when we get home . . . And if our father killed our mother? A blow with a stone is all it would take! What would we do?"

"Me, I pray every time I go to the well because it's so deep. I tell myself that if somebody pushed me in, no one would know where I was. You could die down there, nobody will come looking for you."

That well was my great terror, and my mother's, too. I could feel it. And I was afraid in the ravines when I led the goats and the sheep back. The idea would loom up in me that my father could be hiding somewhere and that he was going to push me into the void. It would be easy for him to do, and I would be dead at the bottom of the ravine. They could even pile up a few stones on top of me and I would be in the ground and I'd be left there to rot.

The possibility of our mother dying preoccupied us more than the death of a sister because there were always other sisters. Our mother was often beaten just as we were. Sometimes she tried to intervene when my father beat us really viciously, and then he'd turn the blows on her, knocking her down and pulling her by her hair. We lived every day with the possibility of death, day after day.

It could come for no reason, take you by surprise, simply because the father had decided it. Just as my mother had decided to smother the baby girls. She would be pregnant, then she wasn't, and nobody asked any questions.

We didn't have any real contact with other girls in the village except to say hello and good-bye. We were never together, except for weddings. And the conversations were banal, about the food, about the bride, about other girls who we thought were pretty or ugly, or maybe about a woman we thought was lucky because she was wearing makeup.

"Look at that one, she's plucked her eyebrows . . ."

"She has a nice haircut."

"Oh, look at that one, she's wearing shoes!"

This would be the richest girl in the village, she wore embroidered slippers. The rest of us went into the fields barefoot, where we got thorns in our feet and would have to sit on the ground to take them out. My mother didn't have any shoes, either, and my sister Noura was married barefoot. The wedding ceremony consisted of only a few sentences exchanged. I was present at only two or three of these ceremonies.

It was unthinkable to complain about being beaten because that was just the way it was. There was no question about a baby being alive or dead, unless a woman had just given birth to a son. If this son was alive, then glory to her and to the family. If he was dead, they wept over him and the misfortune that had befallen her and her family. The males counted, not the females.

When I disappeared from my village later, my mother must not have been forty years old. She had given birth to fourteen children and only five were living. Had she smothered all the others? Nobody really cared because it was customary. I never knew what became of the baby girls after my mother smothered them. Did they bury them somewhere? Did they become food for the dogs? My mother would dress in black, my father also. Every birth of a girl was like a burial in the family. It was always considered the mother's fault if she produced only girls. My father thought so and so did the whole village.

In my village, if the men had to choose between a girl and a cow, they would choose the cow. My father repeated endlessly how we girls were not good for anything: A cow gives milk and produces calves. What do you do with milk and calves? You sell them and bring the money home, which means a cow does something for the family. But a girl? What does the family get from her? Nothing. What do sheep bring to us? Wool. You sell the wool and you get money. The lamb grows up, it makes other lambs, still more milk, you make cheese, you sell it and you bring home money. A cow and a sheep are more valuable than a girl. And we girls knew this very well because the cow, the sheep, and the goat were treated much better than we were and they were never beaten!

And we also knew that a girl is a problem for her father because he is always afraid of not being able to marry her off. And once she's married it is a cause for misery and shame if she leaves her husband, who's mistreating her, and dares come back to her parents' house. But as long as she is not married, the father is afraid that she'll stay an old maid and the village will gossip. For the whole family that is a terrible embarrassment because if an unmarried girl walks in the street with her father and mother, everyone looks at her and makes fun of her. If she's more than twenty years old and still in her parents' house, it is not normal. Everyone observes the rule of marrying the eldest daughter first and the rest in the order of their ages. But after the age of twenty, nobody makes allowances. A girl is expected to be married. I don't know how this worked in the big cities of my country but that's the way it was in my village.

Hanan?

There was an abiding fear of death and of the iron door. It was the fear of the submissive surviving girls. My brother, Assad, on the other hand, would leave for school with a satchel. He also went horseback riding and went walking. He did not eat with us. He grew up as a man should grow up, free and proud, and was served like a prince by the girls of the house. Assad was handsome and I adored him like a prince. I heated the water for his bath when he was still small and I washed his hair. I took care of him as you would a priceless treasure. I knew nothing of his life outside the house and I was ignorant of what he learned in that school, and of what he saw and did in town. We waited for him to come of age and marry because marriage is the only thing that has any real importance in a family, that and the birth of a son!

There was only a year between us, which gave me the opportunity to be close to him while he was still a child. In my family we were as close to each other in age as it was possible to be. I don't have any memory of playing with him as children of that age do in Europe, and by the age of fourteen or fifteen he was already a man and he drifted away from me.

I think he married very early, probably at about the age of seventeen. He had also become violent. My father hated him but I did not know the reason. Perhaps he was too much like him. He was afraid of losing his power to a son who had become an adult. I don't know the origin of the anger between them, but one day I saw my father take a basket and fill it with stones, and then go up on the terrace and hurl them at Assad's head, as if he wanted to kill him.

When he married, Assad lived with his wife in a part of our house. He pushed an armoire against the connecting door to keep my father from coming in. I quickly understood that the violence of the men of my village comes from way back in our history. The father passes it to the son who transmits it in his turn, over and over.

I haven't seen my family in twenty-five years, but if by some chance I were to come across my brother, I would like to ask him just one question: *Where is the sister, the one I call Hanan, who disappeared?* Hanan—I can see her—a beautiful girl, very dark and prettier than me, with thick hair and heavy eyebrows that joined above her eyes, and who was more mature physically. I remember that Kainat is sweet and good, but a little too heavy, and that Hanan has a different personality, is a little abrupt in her manner but yet submissive like the rest of us. Hanan's not fat but you sensed she could become strong and perhaps a little chubby. She's not a thin girl like me. When she comes to help us pick olives, she works and moves slowly. This wasn't usual in the family; you walked fast, you worked fast, you ran to obey to bring out the animals and bring them back. Rather than being active, she was dreamy and never very attentive to what was being said to her. When we'd be picking olives, for example, my fingers would already be sore from collecting a whole bowlful but she wouldn't have even filled the bottom of hers. I would go back to help her because if she was always behind everybody else she was going to get into trouble with my father. I see us all in a row in the olive grove. We move forward in a line, stooped over and moving with the rhythm of the picking. The movement has to be quick. As soon as the hand is full, you throw the olives into the basin and you keep going like that until the olives are almost overflowing the basin. Then you put them into the big cloth sacks. Each time I come back to my place, I see Hanan is still behind, as if moving in slow motion. She is really very different from the others. I have no recollection of speaking with her or of being especially involved with her, except for helping her with the olive picking when it was needed. Or twisting her thick hair into a big braid, as she was supposed to do for me. I don't see her with us in the stable or leading the cows, or shearing the sheep's wool. She spent most of her time in the kitchen helping my mother, which may be why she has disappeared somewhat from my memory.

But I have counted and recounted, forcing myself to get us in the right birth order: Noura, Kainat, Souad, Assad, and . . . ? My fourth sister is not there; I have lost even her first name. Eventually it would happen that I didn't even know anymore who was born before whom. I was sure about Noura, sure about Assad, but then I'd get the rest of us mixed up. As for the one I call Hanan, the worst thought for me is that for years I didn't even ask myself anymore about her disappearance. I forgot her profoundly, as if a door had closed on this sister of my blood, making her completely invisible to my memory, which was already jumbled.

Some time ago, however, a brutal image arose in my mind, an atrocious vision came into my head. Someone, in a gathering of women, showed me a photo of a dead girl lying on the ground who had been strangled with a black telephone cord. I had the feeling of having already seen something similar. This photo made me very uneasy, not only because of this unfortunate murdered girl, but because I was groping in a fog to "see" something that concerned me. And, strangely, the next day my memory returned with a start. I was there and I had witnessed this scene! I now knew when and how this sister, Hanan, had disappeared!

Since that moment of recognition I live with this new nightmare in my head, which sickens me. Every precise memory, every scene of my past existence that brutally returns makes me sick. I would like to forget all these horrible things completely, and for more than twenty years I unconsciously succeeded in doing just that. But to bear witness to my life as a child and a woman in my country, I am forced to plunge into these horrible memories, as if to the bottom of that well that made me so afraid. And all these bits of my past that rise to the surface seem to me now so terrible that I have trouble believing them.

When I'm alone, I sometimes ask myself if I really lived these things. I am still here, I survived them. Other women have lived through these things and they, too, are still living in the world. I would like to forget, but we survivors who can speak out are so few that it is my duty to bear witness and to do so I must relive these nightmares.

As for the vision of Hanan, I am in the house and I hear shouting. Then I see my sister sitting on the ground, flailing her arms and legs, and my brother, Assad, leaning over her, his arms on either side of her. He is strangling her with the telephone cord. I remember this scene as if it took place yesterday. I was standing in front of my two little sisters to shield and protect them. We pressed

26

ourselves against the wall to try to make ourselves disappear. I hold them by the hair so they won't move. Assad must have seen us or heard me enter. He yells: "*Rouhi! Rouhi!* Get out! Get out!"

I run to the cement stairs that lead to the bedrooms dragging my two sisters. One of the little ones is so afraid that she stumbles and hurts her leg, but I make her keep going. My whole body is trembling as I lock us in the room and console the little one. I try to care for her knee and we stay there for a long time, all three of us, not making a sound. I can't do anything, absolutely nothing but keep quiet, with this vision of horror in our heads, of my brother strangling our sister. She must have been using the telephone and he came up behind to strangle her. She is dead; I'm convinced she is dead. That day she was wearing white pants, with a shirt that went to the knees. She was barefoot. I saw her legs kick and I saw her arms strike my brother in the face as he shouted at us, "Get out!"

The telephone was black, I think. How long had this telephone been in the house? There can't have been many of them in the village at that time. My father had modernized the house. We now had a bathroom with hot water and a telephone. It was kept on the floor in the main room and it had a very long cord. She must have been trying to use it, but I don't know whom she was calling or why. I don't know what I was doing before that, or where I was, or what Hanan might have done for her part, but nothing in her behavior that I know of justifies my brother's strangling her. *I don't know what is happening.*

I stayed in the bedroom with the little girls until my mother came back. She and my father had gone out, leaving us alone with Assad. For a long time I tried to understand why there was nobody else in the house but him and us. Then the memories become intertwined.

That day, my parents went to see my brother's wife at her parents' house, where she had taken refuge because she was pregnant and he had beaten her. That's why my brother was alone with us in our house. And he must have been furious, like all men, to be insulted like this. As usual, I had only snatches of information about what was happening. A girl is not present at family meetings when there are conflicts. She's kept out of the way. I learned later that my sister-in-law had a miscarriage, and I suppose my parents accused my brother of being responsible. But that day there was no link between the two events. What was Hanan doing on the telephone? It was used very little. I myself used it only two or three times to speak with my older sister, my aunt, or my brother's wife. If Hanan was calling someone, it had to be somebody in the family. When my parents came home, my mother spoke to Assad. I see her crying, but I know she is just pretending. I've become a realist and have come to understand how things happen in my land. I know why they kill girls and how that happens. It is decided at a family gathering and on the fatal day, the parents are never present. Only the one who has been picked to do the killing is with the girl who is the intended victim.

My mother wasn't really crying. She was just pretending to cry! She certainly knew why my brother had strangled my sister. If not, why go out that very day with my father and my older sister Noura? Why leave us alone in the house with Assad? What I don't know is the reason for Hanan's condemnation. She must have committed a sin but I have no idea what it was. Did she go out alone? Or was she seen speaking to a man? Was she denounced by a neighbor? It doesn't take much at all before a girl is seen by everyone as

28

a *charmuta*, who has brought shame to the family and who must now die to wash clean the honor not only of her parents and her brother, but of the entire village!

My sister was more mature than I, even if she was younger in age. She must have committed an imprudence that I wasn't aware of. Girls don't exchange confidences. They're too afraid of speaking, even among sisters. I know something about this, because I also kept silent.

I loved my brother very much. All the sisters loved him because he was the only man of the family, the only protector after my father. If the father dies, he will run the house, and if he should die, and only women are left, the family is lost. No more sheep, no more land, no more anything. Losing an only son and brother is the worst thing that can happen to a family. How can you live without a man? It is the man who makes the law and protects us; it is the son who takes the place of the father and marries off his sisters.

As I have said, Assad was violent like my father. He was a murderer, but that word doesn't have any meaning in my village when it comes to having a woman killed. It is the duty of the brother, the brother-in-law, or the uncle to preserve the family's honor. They have the right of life and death over their women. If the father or the mother says to the son: "Your sister has sinned, you must kill her," he does it for the sake of honor and because it is the law.

Let me tell you a bit about him. Assad was our adored brother. He loved to ride horses. One day, the horse slipped and Assad fell. I remember that so well. We cried and cried. I ripped my dress with grief and I tore my hair. Fortunately, it wasn't serious and we took care of him. And still today I can't fully accept that Assad is a murderer. The image of my strangled sister is a recurring nightmare now, but at the time I don't think I could really hold it against him. What he did was the accepted custom. He must have agreed that he had to do it out of duty, because it was necessary for the whole family. And I loved him anyway.

I don't know what they did with Hanan's body but she disappeared from the house. I forgot about her but I don't understand very well why that was. Besides fear, there is of course the logic of my life at that time, the customs, the law, everything that makes us live these things as though they are normal. They only become crimes and horrors when you are elsewhere, in the West or in other countries where the laws are different. I myself was also supposed to die. And to have survived the customary punishment of my land by a miracle was very disturbing to me for a long time. Now I can see that the shock of what happened to me made me "forget" about other events in my life. At least, that's what a psychiatrist told me.

So this is how Hanan disappeared from my life and from my memories for a long time. Maybe she was buried with the other babies. Maybe they burned her, buried her under a pile of debris or in a field. Perhaps they gave her to the dogs? I don't know. When I talk about my life there, I can see in people's expressions the difficulty they have understanding. They ask me questions that seem logical to them: "Did the police come?" "Wasn't anyone concerned about a person's disappearance?" "What did the people in the village say?"

Rarely did I see the police. It's nothing if a woman disappears. And the villagers agree with the men's law. If you don't kill a girl who has dishonored her family, the people in the village will reject this family, and nobody will speak to the family or do business with them and the family will have to leave!

Seen from the point of view of my life now, my sister endured a fate worse than mine. But she is also lucky because she is dead. At least, she isn't suffering. I still hear my sister's cries in my ears, so loudly did she scream! Kainat and I were afraid for a long time. Every time we saw my father, my brother, or my brother-in-law, we were afraid he would do something to us. And sometimes we couldn't sleep. I would wake up frequently at night. I felt a permanent threat over me. Assad was always angry and violent. He wasn't allowed to go to see his wife. She had gone directly to her parents' house when she left the hospital because he had beaten her too severely. But she later returned to live with him anyway; it's the law. She gave him other children, fortunately sons. We were proud of him, we loved him so much, even if he frightened us. What I don't understand is that I adored my brother as much as I hated my father, although in the end they were very alike.

If I had gotten married in my village, and had given birth to girls, Assad might have been given the order to strangle one of my daughters. I would have acted like all the other women and would have submitted without revolting. It's unbearable to think and say such a thing here in my other life, but there, that's the way it is. I now see things very differently because I "died" in my village and I was reborn in Europe. But I still love my brother. It is like the root of an olive tree that can't be torn out, even if the tree has fallen.

The Green Tomato

I would clean out the stable every morning. It was very large and the odor was strong. When I had finished cleaning, I would leave the door open to air it out. It was very damp and with the heat of the sun the inside of the stable was steamy. The buckets would be filled with manure, and I would carry them on my head into the garden to dry. A portion of this manure from the horses was used for fertilizing the garden. My father said it was the best fertilizer. The sheep droppings were used for the bread oven. When they were thoroughly dried I would sit on the ground and work them by hand into little cakes that I would put in a pile for feeding the oven.

The sheep would be led into the fields early in the morning, and we would return to bring them back to the stable around eleven o'clock when the sun would be too hot. The sheep would eat and sleep. I would also go to the house to eat, some oil in a bowl, warm bread, some tea, olives and fruit. In the evening, there was chicken, lamb, or rabbit. We ate meat almost every day with rice and semolina that we made ourselves. All the vegetables came from the garden.

As long as the heat lasted in the garden, I would work in the house. I prepared the dough for the bread and also fed the smallest lambs. I would take them by the skin of their necks, the way you hold a cat, and I would bring them up to the mother's udder for them to nurse. There were always several of them so I would take care of one after the other. When one had nursed enough I would put it back in its place until they had all been fed. Then I would go take care of the goats, which were kept separate in the stable. The two horses had their own corner and the cows, too. This stable was really immense and held a good sixty sheep and at least forty goats. The horses were always outside in the fields and were brought back in only at night. They were for the use of my father and brother to ride, never for us. When the stable work was finished, I could leave the door open for ventilation because there was a heavy wooden gate that kept the animals from going out.

When the sun was lower in the sky, I had to tend the garden. There were many tomatoes that had to be picked almost every day when they were ripe. Once, by mistake, I picked a green tomato. I haven't forgotten it, that tomato! I often think about it now in my kitchen. It was half yellow and half red and was beginning to ripen. I had thought about hiding it when I brought it back to the house, but it was already too late, my father had already arrived. I knew that I shouldn't have picked it but I was working too fast with both hands. Because I was expected to work very fast, my movements were mechanical, my fingers turned around the tomato plant, left right left right down to the bottom. And the last one, the one that had received the least sun, was in my hand before I knew it. And it was there, very visible in the basin. My father shouted: "You fool! You see what you've done? You picked a green tomato!

Majmouma!" He struck me and then he crushed the tomato over my head and the seeds fell on me. "Now you're going to eat it!" He crammed it into my mouth and he rubbed my face with the rest of the tomato. I'd thought that an unripe tomato might be eaten, but it was acid, very bitter, and smelled bad. I was forced to swallow it. I couldn't eat anything after that because my stomach was upset. But he pushed my head into my plate and made me eat my meal, almost like a dog. He had me by the hair. I felt sick but I couldn't move. My half sister made fun of me and laughed. She received such a slap that she spit out what she had in her mouth and started to cry. The more I said my head hurt the more he persisted in crushing my face into the semolina. He emptied the whole plate and made little balls of semolina that he forced into my mouth, he was that enraged. Then he wiped his hands on a napkin, threw it at my head, and went and calmly settled himself in the shade on the veranda. I wept as I cleaned off the platter. I had food all over my face, my hair, and in my eyes. And I swept up as I did every day to pick up the tiniest grain of semolina that had escaped my father's hand.

Even though for years I forgot events as important as the disappearance of one of my sisters, I never forgot this green tomato, and the humiliation of being treated as less than a dog. And to see him there calmly sitting in the shade, napping like a king after my almost daily thrashing, was the worst of all. He was the symbol of an enslavement that was taken for granted, that I accepted, bending my back and lowering my head under the blows, like my sisters and my mother. But today I understand my hatred. I would have wished him to suffocate in his head scarf.

This was everyday life. Toward four o'clock, we brought out the sheep and the goats until sunset. My sister walked beside the ones at the head of the flock, and I always took the rear position with a cane to move the animals along and especially to scare the goats. They were always agitated, ready to take off anywhere. Once we were in the field there was a little tranquility because it was only us and the flock. I would take a watermelon and tap it on a stone to open it. We were afraid of being caught when we returned because our dresses were spotted with sugar juice. We would wash them on ourselves in the stable before our parents saw us. Since it wasn't possible to take off the dresses, it was lucky they dried very fast.

The sun would take on a special yellow and then fade on the horizon, the sky changing from blue to gray. We would have to return before nightfall, and since night came very quickly, we had to move as fast as the sun, scurry close to the walls, and then the iron door would clang shut on us again.

When it was time to milk the cows and the sheep, a big milk can was put under the cow's belly, and I sat on a stool almost at ground level. I would take a cow's hoof and squeeze it between my legs so the animal wouldn't move and so the milk wouldn't go anywhere but into the bucket. If there was a puddle of milk on the ground, even a few drops, it would mean trouble for me! My father would slap me and shout at me that he'd lost a cheese! The cow's tits were very big, very hard because they were swollen with milk, and my hands were small. My arms would hurt since I'd spent a lot of time pulling and I was exhausted. Once, when there were six cows in the stable, I fell asleep hanging on the bucket, the cow's hoof between my legs. As luck had it my father arrived and shouted, "Charmuta! Whore!" He dragged me on the ground in the stable by the hair and I caught a whipping with a belt. I cursed this wide leather belt that he always wore around his waist with another smaller one. The small one jangled loudly. He would swing it around with force, holding it by one end like a rope. When he used the big one, he had to fold it in two, it was too heavy. I begged him and I cried in pain, but the more I said it hurt the more he struck me and called me a whore.

I would still be crying in the evening, when it was time for the meal. My mother could see that he had given me a bad beating that evening but if she tried to question me, he started to hit her, too, telling her it wasn't any of her business, that she didn't need to know why I'd been beaten because I knew the reason.

On an ordinary day in the house, there would be a slap or a kick on the pretext that I wasn't working fast enough or that the water for the tea had taken too long to heat. Sometimes I succeeded in dodging the bang on the head but not often. I don't remember if my sister Kainat was beaten as much as I was but I think so because she was every bit as afraid. I've kept this reflex of working very fast and walking fast, as if a belt were permanently waiting for me. A donkey is moved along the road by being rapped with a stick. It was the same for us, except that my father would strike us much harder than he would have struck a donkey. I have also been struck the next day, just on principle, so I shouldn't forget the licking of the previous day. All that so I would continue to move along without falling asleep, like the donkey on the road.

Mention of a donkey makes me think of another memory concerning my mother. I can see myself taking the flock to graze as usual, and coming very quickly back to the house to clean the stable. My mother is with me and she hurries me because we have to go and pick figs. The crates had to be loaded onto the donkey's back and we had to walk a long way beyond the village. I'm not able to place this story in time, except that this morning seems to me very close to the incident of the green tomato. It is the end of the season, because the fig tree we're standing in front of is bare. I tie the donkey to the trunk of this fig tree to keep him from eating the fruit and the leaves that are scattered on the ground.

I begin to pick and my mother says to me: "Pay attention Souad, you stay here with the donkey, you pick up all the figs on the side of the road but you don't go farther than this tree. You don't move from here. If you see your father arrive with the white horse or your brother, or somebody else, you whistle and I'll come quick." She moves off a little on the road to join a man on a horse who is waiting for her. I know him by sight, his name is Fadel. He has a round head, and he's small and strong. His horse is well cared for, very white with a black spot, the tail braided to the end. I don't know if he's married or not.

My mother is cheating on my father with him. I knew it as soon as she said to me: *If somebody else comes, you whistle.* The man on the horse disappears from my view, and my mother, too. I conscientiously pick the figs on the edge of the road. There aren't too many in this spot but I'm not allowed to go looking any farther because if I did I wouldn't be able to see my father or anyone else who might come along.

For some strange reason this story doesn't surprise me. I don't remember feeling afraid of anything. Perhaps because my mother had organized her plan so well. The donkey is tied to the trunk of a bare fig tree. He can't reach anything to eat it, not leaves or fruit. So I don't need to watch him as I would in the height of the season and I can work alone. I take ten steps in one direction, ten in the other, picking up the figs lying on the ground to put them in the crates. I have a good view of the road looking toward the village; I can see in the distance anyone who'd be approaching and whistle in time. I don't see Fadel or my mother anymore but I guess they're about fifty steps away, hidden somewhere in the field. So if someone were to arrive on the scene she could always make them believe that she went off for a moment for urgent personal business. A man, even my father or brother, would never ask an indecent question about such a thing. It would be shameful.

I'm not alone for very long. The crate doesn't have much in it when they arrive separately. My mother comes out of the field. I see Fadel get back on his horse; he misses the saddle the first time because the horse is tall. He has a pretty wooden riding whip, very finely made, and he smiles at Mama before riding off. I pretend to have seen nothing. The whole thing happened very quickly. They made love somewhere in the field, sheltered by the grass, or they were simply talking together, I don't want to know. It's not my business to ask what they did, or look surprised. My mother will not confide in me. And she knows, too, that I won't say anything, quite simply because I'm an accomplice, and I'd be beaten to death, too. My father only knows how to beat women and make them work to get money. So if my mother goes to make love with another man on the pretext of gathering figs, I'm not bothered by it. She has good reason.

Now we have to gather the figs very quickly so the crates will be full enough to justify the time we've spent here. Otherwise my father is going to ask: "You bring back empty crates. What were you doing all that time?" And I'll get the belt. We are rather far from the village. My mother gets on the donkey, her legs straddling the animal's neck, very close to his head so as not to crush the figs. I walk in front to guide the animal on the road and we set off with a heavy load.

We soon encounter an elderly woman, all alone with a donkey, who is also gathering figs. Since she is elderly, she can be out alone. As we catch up with her, my mother greets her and we continue on our way together. This road is very narrow and difficult, full of holes, bumps, and stones. In places it rises steeply and the donkey has trouble advancing with his load. At one point he stops dead at the top of a slope before a big snake and refuses to go on. My mother strikes him and encourages him but he wants no part of it. Instead he tries to move back, his nose trembling with fear, like me. I detest snakes. And because the incline is really very steep, the crate starts to dislodge on his back and almost overturns. Fortunately, the woman who is with us seems not at all afraid of the snake, however enormous it is. I don't know how she does it, but I see it roll up and twist. She must have struck it with her walking stick, and the big snake slithers into the ditch. The donkey is then willing to move on.

There were a lot of snakes around the village, small ones and big ones. The snakes would even nest in the house, in the storeroom between the sacks of rice, or in the piles of hay in the stable. We would see them every day and we were very afraid of them the way we fear grenades. Ever since the war with the Jews, grenades were all over the place. You didn't know if you were going to die when you put your foot down. In any case, I heard them talk about it at home, when my father's father would come for a visit, or my uncle. My mother warned us about these grenades, they were almost invisible in the middle of pebbles and stones, and I watched constantly ahead of me for fear of coming across one. I don't personally remember having seen one but I know that the danger was

40

always there. It was better not to pick up a stone and to pay attention to where you stepped.

My father wasn't there when we got home. It was a relief because we had lost time and it was already ten o'clock. At that hour the sun is high, the heat strong, and the figs at risk of shriveling and softening. They had to be in good condition and carefully prepared for my father to be able to sell them at the market. I liked preparing the crates of figs. I would choose beautiful fig leaves, big green ones to carpet the bottom of the crates. Then I would place the figs delicately, in neat rows like beautiful jewels, and put large leaves on top to protect them from the sun. It was the same preparation for the grapes: We cut them with a scissors and cleaned them carefully; there couldn't remain a single damaged grape or a dirty leaf. I also lined these crates with vine leaves and covered them the same way as the figs so the grapes would stay fresh.

There was also the season for cauliflower, zucchini, eggplant, tomatoes, and squash, and my father sold the cheese that I was assigned to make. I would pour the milk into a large metal bucket. I would skim off the yellow fat that formed on the edges, and the cream, which I set aside for making *laban*, which was sold in separate packets for Ramadan. The *laban* were put into large buckets for my father, who made up the packets with heavy plastic so that the product wouldn't spoil. It was my job to label them in Arabic: LABAN.

With the *halib*, the milk, I made yogurt and cheese by hand, using a white transparent cloth and an iron bowl. First I would fill the bowl to the top so all the cheeses were the same height; then I turned them into the cloth, tied a knot, and squeezed very hard so the liquid would run into a receptacle. When there was no more liquid, they were placed on a big gilded platter and covered with a cloth so the sun and the flies wouldn't damage them. I would wrap them then in white packets that my father also marked. My father went to the market almost every day during the fruit-and-vegetable season, and twice a week with the cheeses and the milk.

My father would not get behind the wheel of the van until it was completely loaded, and woe to us if we hadn't finished in time. He would get in front with my mother and I would be wedged in between the crates in back. It was a good half hour's ride, and when we arrived I would see big buildings. It was the city, a pretty, very clean city. There were stoplights to control the auto traffic. I remember a shop window with a mannequin in a bride's dress. I twisted my head to be able to see the shops for as long as possible. I had never seen anything like that, because I wasn't allowed to walk about and certainly could not look in the shops.

I would have loved to visit this city, but when I saw girls walking on the sidewalk wearing short dresses and with bare legs, I was ashamed. If I had encountered them close up I would have spit on their path. They were *charmuta* and I thought it was disgusting. They were walking all alone, without parents next to them. I thought to myself that they would never be married. No man would ever ask for them because they had shown their legs and they were made up with lipstick. And I didn't understand why they weren't locked in. Were these girls beaten the way I was? Locked up like me? Slaves like me? Did they work the way I did? I wasn't allowed to move an inch from my father's van. He supervised the unloading of the crates, collected the money, and then gave a sign, as if to a donkey, for me to climb in and hide myself inside, with the only pleasures being a moment without any work to do, and catching sight of the inaccessible boutiques through the crates of fruits and vegetables. I understand now that life in my village hadn't changed since my mother was born, and her mother before her, and still farther back.

The market was very large with a sort of roof that was covered with vines and that provided some shade for the fruit. It was very pretty. When everything had been sold, my father was very happy. He would go alone to see the vendor before the market closed, and he brought back the money, which I could see in his hand. He always counted it several times and then put it in a small cloth sack that was tied with a string and hung around his neck. It was with this money from the market that he was able to modernize the house.

When my sister went to the market with my parents, I would go fetch water for cleaning the courtyard, which would be dried by the sun. And I made things to eat. Sitting on the ground I put the flour in a large flat plate with water and salt, and I worked it with my hand. The dough would rest under a white cloth, slowly rising. I would then go stoke the bread oven to get it really hot. The bake house had a wooden roof and was as big as a small house. Inside, the iron oven was always burning. The live coals stayed hot but the fire had to be stoked before we cooked on it, especially before making bread.

I loved making the bread. So that the dough wouldn't stick to my hands, I plunged them into flour and I caressed this white soft dough. Rising dough is a magnificent thing. I would make a hole in the dough to make it attractive before putting it in the oven. I made a big pancake, a beautiful round loaf, and a flat one that always had to have the same shape. If it didn't, my father would throw it in my face. After the bread was baked, I would clean the oven and pick up the cinders. When that was finished, my hair, my face, my eyebrows and eyelashes were gray with dust, and I would shake myself off like a wet dog.

One day, I was in the house and smoke was seen coming from the roof of the bake house. I ran with my sister to see what was happening and we heard them shouting "Fire!" My father came with water. There were flames and everything burned. Inside the bake house there were what looked like blackened goat droppings. I had forgotten a bread inside the oven and had not carefully cleaned the cinders. A coal was left, which started the fire. It was my fault. I shouldn't have forgotten this piece of bread or forgotten to stir up the cinders with a piece of wood to take out the live embers. I was responsible for the fire in the bread oven, which was the worst of catastrophes.

As expected, my father beat me harder than he ever had. He kicked me, beat my back with a cane, caught me by the hair, pushed me to my knees, and forced my face into the cinders, fortunately only warm by now. I was suffocating and spitting because the ash went into my nose and mouth. My eyes were reddened. He made me eat cinders to punish me. I was weeping when he released me, all black and gray with my eyes red as tomatoes. It was a very grave fault, and if my sister and mother hadn't been there, I believe my father would have thrown me into the fire before it had been extinguished.

The oven had to be rebuilt with bricks and the work took a long time. Every single day I got an insult, a mean word. I would slink to the stable bent low and I would sweep the courtyard with my head lowered. I think my father really detested me. But this one mistake aside, I always worked really well. I would do all the laundry of the house in the afternoon before night fell. I would beat the sheepskins, sweep, cook, feed the animals, clean out the stable. The moments of rest were so rare. When we weren't working for ourselves, we would help the other villagers and they did the same for us.

We were never out at night. But my father and mother would often go out to the neighbors, to the houses of friends. My brother would also go out, but not the rest of us. We didn't have any friends, and my older sister never came to see us. The only person outside the family whom I saw sometimes was a neighbor, Enam. She had a spot in her eye and people made fun of her and everyone knew that she had never been married.

From the terrace I could see the villa of the rich people. They would be out there with lights on, and I would hear them laugh. They ate outside, even late at night. But in our house we were locked up like rabbits in our rooms. In the village, I remember only this rich family, not very far from our house, and Enam, the old maid always alone, sitting outside in front of her house. The only distraction for us girls was the trip to the market in the van.

There were several girls more or less of the same age in the village and they would put us all in a bus to be taken to pick cauliflowers in a big field. I remember so well this huge field of cauliflowers. It was so big you couldn't see the end of it and you felt you would never get it all picked. The driver was so small that he sat on a cushion to be able to see over the steering wheel. He had a funny small round head with close-cropped hair.

All day long we cut cauliflowers on all fours, all the girls in a row as usual, and supervised by an older woman with a stick. There was no question of loafing. We piled the cauliflowers up in a big truck. At the end of the day, the truck stayed there and we got back into the bus to return to the village. There were many orange trees on either side of the road, and because we were very thirsty the driver stopped and told us to go get an orange for each of us and to come right back. "One orange and *halas!*" which meant "one but not two!"

All the girls ran back to the bus and the driver, who had parked on a little side road, backed up. Then he suddenly turned off the motor, got out, and started to yell so loudly that all the girls got out of the bus, frantic. He had run over one of the girls. A wheel of the bus had run over her head. As I was just in front, I bent down, I tried to raise her head by her hair thinking she was still alive. But her head remained stuck to the ground and I passed out from fright.

The next thing I remember, I was in the bus, sitting on the knees of the woman who was supervising us. The driver was stopping before every house to let the girls off as we weren't allowed to return alone even in the village. When I got off in front of our house the supervisor explained to my mother that I was sick. Mama put me to bed and gave me something to drink. She was good to me that night because the woman had explained it all to her. She had to explain the accident to each mother and the driver waited. I wondered if he wanted to be sure that everyone was told the same thing.

It's odd that it happened to this particular girl. When we were gathering the cauliflowers, she was always in the middle of the row, never on the edges. Among us, when a girl is always protected like this by the other girls it means that she might run away. And I had noticed that this girl was always surrounded, that she wasn't able to switch places in the line, and no one spoke to her. It was forbidden to even look at her because she was *charmuta*, and if we did speak to her they would treat us, too, as *charmuta*. Did the driver deliberately run over her? The rumor lasted a long time in the village. The police came to question us and brought us together in the bus to the field where it had happened. There were three policemen, and that was really something for us to see men dressed in uniform. We could not look them in the eye and we had to be very respectful. We were very impressed. We showed them the exact spot. I bent down. There was a dummy head on the ground and I raised it with my hand as I had done with the girl. They said to me: "*Halas, halas, halas . . .*" And that was it.

We got back in the bus. The driver was weeping! He drove fast and wildly. The bus bounced on the road and I remember that the supervisor held her chest with both hands because her breasts were bouncing, too. The driver was put in prison. For us and for the whole village this was not an accident.

For a very long time after this I was sick. I kept seeing myself raising the crushed head of this girl and I was afraid of my parents because of everything they were saying about her. They said she was *charmuta*. She must have done something bad but I don't know what it was. I didn't sleep at night, I kept seeing this crushed head and hearing the sound of the tires when the bus backed up. Never will I forget this girl. Despite all the sufferings I have endured myself, this image has stayed with me. She was the same age as I, with short hair, a very pretty haircut. It was also bizarre that she had short hair. The girls in the village never cut their hair. Why did she? She was different from us, more nicely dressed. What had turned her into a *charmuta*? I never knew. But in my own case, I knew.

As I continued to mature, I waited hopefully to be asked for in marriage. But no one asked for Kainat, and she didn't seem too concerned, as she was already resigned to remaining an old maid. I found this frightful, both for her as well as for me, who had to wait her turn.

I was beginning to feel embarrassed to show myself at the weddings of others for fear of being ridiculed. Being married was the most I could hope for in terms of freedom. But even married, a woman risked her life at the least lapse in her conduct. I remember a woman who had four children. Her husband must have worked in the city, because he always had on a jacket. When I would see him in the distance he was always walking very fast, his shoes kicking up a storm of dust behind him. His wife's name was Souheila, and one day I heard my mother say that the village was telling stories about her. People thought she was involved with the owner of the store because she went there frequently to buy bread, vegetables, and fruit. Maybe she didn't have a big garden like ours or maybe she was seeing this man secretly, as my mother had done with Fadel. One day my mother said that her brothers had gone into her house and cut off her head. And that they had left the body on the ground and had walked around the village with her head. She also said that when her husband returned from his job he was happy to learn that his wife was dead since she'd been suspected of something with the store owner. But she wasn't very pretty and she already had four children.

I didn't see these men walk through the village with their sister's head, I only heard the story from my mother. I was already mature enough to understand but I wasn't afraid, perhaps because I hadn't seen anything myself. It seemed to me that in my family nobody was *charmuta*, that these things weren't happening to me.

This woman had been punished for her violation of the rules, this was normal. It was certainly more normal than a girl my age being crushed to death on the road.

I didn't realize that simple gossip based on the neighbors' assumptions, or lies even, could turn any woman into a *charmuta* and lead to her death, for the sake of the honor of the others. It is what is called a crime of honor, *Jamirat el Sharaf*, and for the men of my region it is not considered a crime.

The Bride's Blood

Hussein's parents came to ask for Noura and they returned to discuss it several times. In our land, a girl is sold into marriage for gold. So Hussein's parents brought the gold, which they displayed in a pretty gilded dish, and Hussein's father said: "There, half for Adnan the father, and the other half for his daughter Noura."

If there isn't enough gold, you go on negotiating. The two shares are important because on the day of the wedding the girl is supposed to show everyone how much gold was given to her father in exchange for his daughter.

It is not for Noura, this heavy gold she will carry the day of her marriage. The number of bracelets, the necklace, the diadem, she needs them for her parents' honor and her own. It is terribly shameful for a girl and her family if she has no jewelry on her wedding day. My father forgot to mention this when he told his daughters that they weren't worth what you get for a sheep. When he sells his daughter, he is owed half the gold! And he can bargain.

This goes on without us, being just between the parents. When the business is concluded, there is no paper to sign; it is the men's word that counts. Only the men's. The women, my mother,

Hussein's mother, have no more right to speak than the future bride. No one else in the family has seen the gold yet, but we all know the marriage has been agreed to because Hussein's family has come to us. But we, the females of the family, must keep to ourselves, out of sight, causing no disturbance of the men's negotiations.

My sister Noura knows a man has come into the house with his parents, so she surely will be married. She is very pleased. She tells me she wants to be able to dress better, pluck her eyebrows, have a family of her own and children. Noura has a pretty face and is timid. She is anxious while the fathers discuss, she would like to know how much gold the family has brought, she prays they will come to an agreement. She doesn't know what her future husband looks like, or how old he is, and she will not ask about these things. It is shameful to ask such questions, even for me who could hide somewhere to see what he looks like. Maybe she's afraid that I'll go and say something to our parents. A few days later, my father summons Noura in my mother's presence and tells her she's going to be married on such and such a day. I wasn't there to hear this because I didn't have the right to be with them.

I shouldn't even say I *didn't have the right*, because rights do not even exist. There are customs. This is the way it is and that is all. If your father points to a corner of the room and tells you to stay in that corner the rest of your life, you won't move from there until you die. If your father places an olive in a plate and tells you that today that's all you'll have to eat, you eat only that olive. It is very difficult to get out of this skin of consenting slave. You're born into it as a female. For all of your childhood, this nonexistence, this obedience to the man and his law, is perpetuated by the father, the mother, the brother, and by the husband once you your-self are married.

When my sister Noura reached this much-hoped-for status, I guess she must have been at least fifteen years old. But maybe I'm mistaken, maybe far off, because as I reflect and try to bring order to my memories, I've realized that my life then had none of the personal landmarks that people in Europe have. No birthday, no photographs; it's more like the life of a small animal that eats, works as fast as possible, sleeps, and is beaten. You know that you are "mature" when you're in danger of drawing down the wrath of society at the least false step. And at this "mature" age, marriage is the next step. Normally, a girl is mature at the age of ten and is married between fourteen and seventeen at the latest. Noura must be approaching the limit.

The family has begun to prepare for the marriage, to alert the neighbors. As the house is not very large, they are going to rent the common courtyard for the reception. It's a very attractive place, a sort of flowering garden where there are grapevines and room for dancing. There is a covered veranda that provides shade and will shelter the bride.

My father picked out the sheep. The youngest lamb is always chosen because the meat is tender and doesn't need to be cooked a long time. If the meat has to cook a long time they say the father is not very well off, that he has picked an old sheep and has not fed his guests well. His reputation in the village will suffer, and his daughter's worse yet. So it is my father who chooses the lamb. He goes into the stable, gets hold of the one he has selected, and drags it into the garden. He ties its hooves to keep it from moving, takes a knife, and with a single stroke cuts its throat. Then he takes the head and twists it a little over a large dish to make the blood flow.

I watch this flowing blood with vague disgust. The lamb's legs are still moving. When my father's task is done, the women come to take care of the meat. They boil water for cleaning the inside of the sheep. The intestines aren't eaten but they're used for something because they're carefully laid aside. Then the animal has to be skinned, and it's my mother who takes care of this delicate task. The skin cannot be damaged; it must remain intact. The sheep is now on the ground, emptied and clean. With her big knife, my mother separates the skin from the meat. She cuts right at the skin and pulls it away with a precise movement. The skin comes away gradually until the entire hide is separated from the body. She will let it dry and will either sell it or keep it. Most of the skins from our sheep are sold. But people don't think much of you if you bring a single sheepskin to the market; you need to bring several to show that you are rich.

At nightfall on this day before the wedding, after the sheep, my mother works on my sister. She takes an old pan, a lemon, a little olive oil, an egg yolk, and some sugar. She dissolves and mixes all of this in the pan and closes herself up in a room with Noura. She is going to remove all of Noura's pubic hair with this preparation. Absolutely every single hair of the genital area must be removed. It must all be bare and clean. My mother says that if by chance you forget a single hair, the man will leave without even looking at his wife and will say she is dirty!

Hair on certain parts of women's bodies is thought of as dirty and I can't stop thinking about this. We don't remove hair from our legs or our underarms, only from the vulva. And also the eyebrows, but to make ourselves more attractive. When hair begins to appear on a girl it is the first sign, with her breasts, that she is becoming a woman. And she will die with her hair, since we will be taken back just as we have been created. And yet all the girls are proud of the idea of having their pubic hair removed. It is the proof that they will belong to a man other than their father. Without hair you really become someone. It seems to me it's more a punishment than anything else because I hear my sister yelling. When she comes out of the room a little crowd of women who were waiting behind the door tap their palms and make their ululations. There is great joy: My sister is ready for her marriage, the famous sacrifice of her virginity. After this session, she can go to sleep. The women return to their houses now that they have seen her and verified that everything has gone according to the rules.

At sunrise the next day, the food is prepared in the courtyard. Everyone must see the food being prepared and count the number of dishes. And especially you can't afford to spoil the preparation of a single handful of rice or the whole village will be talking about it. Half the courtyard is given over to the food. There is meat, couscous, vegetables, rice, chickens, and many sweets, cakes that my mother has made with the neighbors' help, because she would never be able to do all this by herself. When the dishes have been displayed for everyone to see, my mother goes with another woman to prepare my sister. The dress is ankle-length and embroidered in front, with cloth buttons. Noura is magnificent when she comes out of the room, covered with gold, beautiful as a flower. She has bracelets, necklaces, and especially, what counts for more than anything for a bride, a diadem! It is made of a ribbon of pieces of gold. Her loose hair has been rubbed with olive oil to make it shine. They will place her on her throne, which is a chair that has been covered with a white cloth and placed on top of a table. Noura is to get up there, where she will sit and be admired by everyone before the arrival of her future husband. All the women jostle each other to get into the courtyard to view the bride, all the while making their ululations.

And the men dance outside. They don't mingle with the women in the courtyard. We're not even allowed to be at the window to watch their dancing. The groom now makes his entrance. The fiancée shyly lowers her head. She is not yet permitted to look at him. This will be the first time she will see what he looks like. I suppose my mother has given her some idea of his appearance, something about his family, his job, his age. But maybe not, maybe all they told her was that his parents brought the right amount of gold.

My mother places a veil on my sister's head. He arrives like a prince, well dressed. He approaches her. Noura keeps her head down under the veil and her hands demurely on her knees to demonstrate her good upbringing. This moment is supposed to represent the essential purpose of my sister's life. I watch with the others, and I envy her. I have always been envious of the eldest, of being able to go everywhere with my mother, while I slogged away in the stable with Kainat. I envy her being the first to leave the house. Every girl would like to be in the bride's place on this day, in a beautiful white dress, covered with gold. Noura is so beautiful. My only disappointment is that she is not wearing shoes. I think it is miserable to be barefoot. I have seen women in the street, going to the market, wearing shoes. Perhaps because the men always wear them, shoes are for me the symbol of freedom. To be able to walk without pebbles and thorns tearing my feet. Noura is barefoot and Hussein is wearing very beautiful polished shoes, which fascinate me.

Hussein comes toward my sister. On the high table, they have installed another chair for him and covered it with a white cloth.

He sits down, raises the white veil, and the ululations resonate in the courtyard. The ceremony is finished. The man has just discovered the face of the woman who has remained pure for him and will give him sons. They remain there, both seated like mannequins. All the others dance, sing, eat, but they don't move. They are brought something to eat and someone covers them with white towels so they don't soil their beautiful clothes. The husband doesn't touch his wife, doesn't kiss her, doesn't take her hand. Nothing is exchanged between them, no gesture of love or tenderness. They are a fixed image of marriage and they sit there like this for a long time.

I don't know anything about this man, his age, if he has brothers or sisters, what he works at, and where he lives with his parents. But he is from the same village. You don't go looking for a woman anywhere but your own village. It's the first time that I, too, have seen this man. We didn't know if he was handsome or ugly, short, tall, fat, blind, awkward, with a twisted mouth, if he had a big nose, or even if he had ears. Hussein is a very attractive man. He is not very tall, he has short curly hair, his face is dark, tanned, a short, rather flat nose with broad nostrils, and he looks well fed. He is good looking. He walks proudly and, at first glance, he doesn't look mean but perhaps he is. I feel it. Now and then, he speaks nervously.

To make it clear that the celebration is ending and the guests are expected to leave, the women sing directly to the husband something that goes like this: "Protect me now. If you don't protect me, you are not a man . . ." And the last obligatory song: "We are not leaving here until you dance." The two of them must dance to conclude the ceremony. The husband helps his wife down—this time he touches her with his finger, she belongs to him now—and they dance together. Some couples don't dance because they are shy. My sister danced well with her husband and it was magnificent for the village.

The husband takes his wife home to his house. It is already nightfall. His father has given him a house; without it he is not a man. Hussein's house is in the village, not very far from my parents' house. The two of them go off on foot alone. We cry as we watch them go. Even my brother is in tears. We weep because she has left us, we weep because we don't know what will happen to her if she's not a virgin for her husband. We are anxious. We will have to wait for the moment when the husband will display the white linen from the balcony or attach it to the window at daybreak so the people can verify officially the presence of the bride's blood. This linen must be visible to everyone, and as many people as possible from the village should come to see it. It is not enough if there are only two or three witnesses. The proof could be contested, you never know.

I remember their house, their courtyard. There was a stone and cement wall around it. Everyone was standing there waiting. All of a sudden my brother-in-law came out with the linen, and that set off the ululations. The men whistle, the women sing, clap their hands, because he has presented the linen. It is a special linen that is placed on the bed for the first night. Hussein tacks it up on the balcony with white clothespins on each side. The wedding is all in white, the pins are white. The blood is red. Hussein acknowledges the crowd with a wave of his hand and goes back in. This is a victory.

The sheep's blood, the blood of the virgin woman, always blood. I remember that on every *Eid*, my father would kill a sheep. The blood would fill a basin, and he would dip a rag in it for painting the entrance door and the tiled floor. To get inside, you had to pass through this door painted in blood. It made me sick. Everything he killed made me sick with fear. When I was a child, I was forced, like the other children, to watch my father kill chickens, rabbits, sheep. My sister and I were convinced he could twist our necks just like a chicken's, drain our blood like the sheep's. The first time I was so terrorized that I hid between my mother's legs so I wouldn't see it, but she made me look. She wanted me to know how my father killed so I would be part of the family, so I wouldn't be afraid. I was always afraid anyway, because the blood represented my father.

The day after the wedding, along with everyone else, I looked at my sister's blood on the white linen. My mother was weeping, and so was I. We cry a lot on this occasion because we want to show our joy and salute the honor of the father who has kept the bride a virgin. And we cry also with relief, for Noura has passed the great test. The only test of her life, except for proving she can produce a son. I hope for the same thing for myself, it's expected. And I'm very happy that she's married, and now it will soon be my turn. It is strange, but at this moment I don't even think about Kainat, as if my sister who is older than me by a year doesn't count. But she has to be married before I can be!

And then the guests go home. We have to dismantle the courtyard. It's the job of the bride's family to wash the serving dishes, clean the courtyard, and there is much to do. Sometimes the neighbor women come to give a hand, but not always.

After her marriage, Noura doesn't come much to the house. She has no reason to go out, because she has to take care of her family. But a short time after the wedding, less than a month in any case, she came back to our house, crying and complaining to

Mama. Since I couldn't ask what had happened, I spied on them from the top of the stairs. Noura showed her bruises. Hussein had struck her so hard that she had bruises on her face, too. She lowered her pants to show her violet thighs, and my mother wept. He must have dragged her on the ground by her hair, all the men do that. But I didn't find out why he had beaten her. Sometimes it's enough if the young bride doesn't know how to cook very well, she forgets the salt, there is no sauce because she forgot to add a little water . . . that's reason enough for a beating. It was my mother Noura complained to, because my father is too violent; he would have sent her back without listening to her. Mama listened to her but didn't console her. She said to her: "He's your husband. It's not serious. You're going to go home."

And Noura went back. Beaten as she was. She returned to her husband who had "corrected" her by beating her with a stick.

There was no choice. Even if he strangled us, there was no choice. Seeing my sister in this condition, I might have felt that marriage was good for nothing more than to be beaten as before. But even at the thought of being beaten, I wanted more than anything in the world to be married. It's a curious thing the destiny of Arab women, in my village in any case. We accept it as natural. No thought of rebelling ever occurs to us. We don't even know what it would mean to revolt. We know how to cry, hide, lie if needed to avoid the stick, but to rebel, never. Quite simply because there's no other place for us to live than in the house of our father or husband. Living alone is inconceivable.

Hussein didn't even come looking for his wife. Anyway, she didn't stay long, my mother was so afraid her daughter wouldn't want to leave! Later, when Noura became pregnant and they were hoping for a boy, she was the princess of her in-laws, of her husband, and of my family. Sometimes I was jealous. She was more important than me in the family. Before she was married, she spent more time with my mother, and afterward they were closer yet. When they would go to gather the wheat together, they took more time because they talked a lot together. They would close themselves up in a room. It was a room that was also used for storing wheat, flour, and olives, and I remember that the door to the room was green. I would pass by it, feeling alone and abandoned, because behind that door my mother was with my sister. They were in there before the wedding when my mother was removing Noura's pubic hair.

I don't know why this door so brutally came into my memory. I went through it almost every day, carrying sacks. Something disturbing happened behind that door, but what? I think I hid between the sacks out of fear. I see myself like a monkey, crouching on my knees in the dark. This room doesn't have much light. I am hiding there, my forehead pressed against the floor. The tile is brown, small brown squares. And my father has painted the spaces in between with white paint. I'm afraid of something. I see my mother. She has a sack over her head. It's my father who has placed this sack on her head. Was it in this room or somewhere else? Is it to punish her? Is it to strangle her? I can't cry out. My father pulls the sack tight behind Mama's head. I see her profile, her nose, against the cloth. With one hand he holds her by the hair and with the other he grips the sack.

He is dressed in black. Something must have happened a few hours earlier? What? My sister came to the house because her husband was beating her. Mama listened to her. Mama should not pity her daughter? She shouldn't cry, she shouldn't try to defend her to my father? It seems to me that memories around that green door are intertwined. My sister's visit and me hiding between the full sacks of wheat, my mother being suffocated by my father with an empty sack. I must have gone in there to hide. It's a habit of mine to hide. In the stable, in this room, or in the armoire in the hallway where they leave the sheepskins to dry before taking them to be sold. They are hung up in there the way they hang them at the market, and I hide inside, even though it's stifling, so I won't be caught. But I don't often hide between the sacks in the storeroom, I'm too afraid snakes will come out. If I was hiding there it's because I feared something bad would happen to me, too.

It is maybe the day my father tried to smother me with a sheepskin, in a room on the ground floor. He wants me to tell him the truth, is Mama cheating on him or not? He folded the wool in two and he pressed it against my face. I would rather die than betray my mother, even if I'd seen her with my own eyes with a man. If I tell the truth he'll kill us both. Even with a knife to my throat, I can't betray her. And I can hardly breathe. Does he let go of me or do I escape? Either way, I run to hide downstairs, behind that green door, between those motionless sacks that appear as monsters. They have always frightened me in this room that is almost dark. I used to dream that my father was going to empty out the wheat at night and fill the sacks with snakes!

There, this is how pieces of my life from before try to find their place in my memory. A green door, a sack, my father who wants to suffocate my mother or me to make me speak, my fear in the dark, and the snakes.

Not long ago, I was emptying a wastebasket into a large garbage bag and a piece of plastic remained caught in the basket. As it fell back into the wastebasket it made a particular sound. I jumped as if a snake had risen up out of this wastebasket. I was trembling and started to cry like a child.

My father knew how to kill a snake. He had a special cane, with two hooks at the end. He would trap it between the hooks so the snake couldn't move, then he would kill it with a stick. If he was capable of immobilizing snakes to kill them, he was also able to put them in the sacks so they would bite me when I plunged my hand in to take out flour. That is why I was so afraid of that green door, which also fascinated me because my mother and sister were inside and were doing the ritual hair removal without me. And because I still had not been asked for officially in marriage. But I heard the rumor when I was barely twelve or thirteen. A family had spoken to my parents about me, officially. There was a man for me somewhere in the village. But I would have to wait. Kainat was ahead of me.

Assad

I was the only one to run to him, to cry when his horse slipped and he fell. I will always have the picture of my brother before me: He was wearing a colorful green shirt, and because it was windy, his shirt billowed behind him. He was magnificent on his horse. I loved my brother so much that this image has never left me.

I think that I was even nicer with him after Hanan's disappearance. I was at his feet. I wasn't afraid of him, I didn't think he would harm me. Perhaps because I was older than he? That we were closer? But he beat us, too, when my father wasn't there. He even attacked my mother once. They were arguing, he pulled her by the hair and she was crying. I see them clearly but don't know the reason for the attack. I always have this great difficulty reassembling the images, or finding their significance. As if my Palestinian memory has been scattered in little pieces in the new life I have had to build in Europe.

It is difficult to understand today, after what my brother did, but at the time, once the terror had passed, I certainly didn't understand that Hanan had died. It's only today, seeing again the scene that has appeared in my memory, that I cannot think otherwise, linking the events together, logically and with perspective. On the one hand, my parents weren't there, and every time an honor crime occurs, meaning that a woman is condemned by her family, the executioner is the only one present. Afterward, I never saw Hanan in the house, never. Assad was crazy with rage that evening, humiliated at being kept away when his wife would be giving birth, demeaned by his in-laws. Had the news of the death of the expected baby arrived by this telephone? Did Hanan speak rudely to him? I don't know. Violence toward women in my family and in our village in general occurred daily! And I loved Assad so much. The more my father detested his son, the more I adored this only brother.

I remember his wedding was an extraordinary celebration. Probably the only memory of real joy in the madness of my past. I must have been about eighteen, already old. I had even refused to go to another wedding because the girls were obviously making fun of me, nudges with the elbow, unpleasant laughter when I passed by. And I cried all the time. Sometimes I was ashamed to go into the village with my flock, afraid of the looks. I wasn't any better than the neighbor with the defective eye whom nobody wanted. My mother allowed me to stay away from the neighbor's wedding, she understood my despair. That's when I dared to speak to my father: "But it's your fault! Let me get married!" But he refused, and he hit me in the head: "Your sister must be married first! Get out!" I said it once but not twice.

But for my brother's wedding the whole family is happy and no one more than I. Her name is Fatma, and I don't understand why she comes from a strange family, from another village. Was there no family near us with a marriageable daughter? My father rented buses to go to the wedding. One for the women and one for the men, the men's in front, of course.

We cross the mountains and every time we pass a sharp bend the women give thanks to Allah with ululations for protecting us from the ravine, which is very dangerous. The countryside resembles a desert, the road isn't paved, it's dry black earth and the wheels of the men's bus stir up a huge cloud of dust in front of us. Everyone is dancing. I have a tambourine between my legs and I accompany the women's ululations. I dance, too, with my scarf, I'm very good at it. Everyone dances, everyone is joyful, the driver is the only one not dancing.

My brother's wedding is a much bigger celebration than my sister's. His wife is young, beautiful, short, and very dark. She is not a child, she is almost Assad's age. In our village, they made a little fun of my father and mother because my brother "has to" marry a girl of mature age, and not known in the village. He should have married a girl younger than himself, it's not normal to marry a girl your own age! And why have to go looking for her outside the village?

She's a very beautiful girl, and she is lucky to have many brothers. My father gave a lot of gold in exchange for her. She wears many jewels. The wedding lasts three entire days of dancing and feasting. I can see myself with my scarf and my tambourine, my heart is happy, I am proud of Assad. He is like a god to us, and this love for him that will not go away is very strange. He is the only one I'm incapable of hating, even if he struck me, even if he beat his wife, even if he became a murderer.

He is in my eyes "Assad the *ahouia*," Assad my brother. *Assad ahouia*. Hello, my brother Assad. I never go to my work without saying to him: "Good morning, my brother Assad." A real devotion. As children we shared many things. Now that he is married and he lives with us with his wife, I continue to serve him. If there is no hot water for his bath, I heat it for him, I clean the bathtub, I wash and put away his underwear. I sew them if needed before I put them away.

It doesn't seem right that I should serve him with so much love because he is like all the other men. Very soon after the wedding, Fatma is beaten and shames him by returning to her parents' house. And contrary to custom, her father and mother don't bring her back to our house by force the very same day. They are perhaps richer, more advanced than us, or as she is their only daughter, they love her more, I don't know. I think that the scenes between my father and brother began because of that. My brother had wanted this woman from another village, he had obliged his father to give a great deal of gold, and the result was that this woman had a miscarriage instead of giving him a son, and she brought dishonor to us by returning to her family. I wasn't present, of course, at the family meetings, and there is nothing in my memory to justify what I'm saying today, but I remember perfectly my father on the terrace with the basket of stones, throwing them one after the other at Assad's head. And that armoire that Assad had wedged against the door of his room to keep my father from entering. Assad perhaps wanted the whole house to himself. He behaved then as if it belonged to him. I think my father didn't want him to have any authority in our house; he felt Assad was taking over his place and his money. My father would often tell my brother that he was still a child. In our culture, it's a serious humiliation to tell a man he is still a child.

Assad rebelled all the more because he was very sure of himself and much too spoiled by us. He was the prince of the house. Assad would shout: "This is my house!" My father wouldn't put up with that. People in the village were asking what foolish thing Fatma might have done, why she went back so often to her father's house. Perhaps she'd been seen with another man? Gossip spreads fast. They said bad things about her but it wasn't true at all, she was a good girl. Unfortunately, if someone says just once that a woman is bad, then the whole village takes it up and it's over for her, she has brought the evil eye on herself.

My mother was unhappy about all of this. Sometimes she would try to calm my father down when he would go after Assad: "Why are you doing this? Let him be!"

"I want to kill him! If you try to protect him, you'll get the same!"

I saw Fatma lying on the ground and my brother kicking her in the back. One day her eye was red and her face all blue. But you couldn't say or do anything. Between the father's violence and the son's, there was nothing for the rest of us to do but hide to avoid being beaten ourselves. Did my brother love his wife? For me love was a mystery. In our culture, you talk of marriage, not of love. Of obedience and total submission, not of a loving relationship between a man and a woman. Only of the obligatory sexual relations with a virgin girl who had been bought for her husband. Where is love?

But I do remember one woman of our village, who lived in the nicest house with her husband and her children. They were known for being rich and having a luxurious house. Their children went to the school. It was a big family because they always married between cousins. They had tiling everywhere; even the path to the outside was tiled. In the other houses, the path was just pebbles or sand, or sometimes it was tarred. In front of their house was a beautiful path, with trees on either side. There was a man who looked after the garden and the courtyard, which was surrounded by a wrought-iron fence that shone like gold. You could see this house from a distance. In our culture, we love everything that shines and shimmers.

If a man has a gold tooth, he must be rich! And if you're rich, everyone must see it. This house was modern and quite new, magnificent from the outside. There were always two or three cars parked in front. I never went inside, of course, but when I passed with my sheep, it made me dream. The owner's name was Hassan. He was a tall gentleman, very tan, and elegant. They were very close, he and his wife, you always saw them together. She was pregnant with twins and was going to give birth. Unfortunately, the birth went badly, the twins lived, but the lady died. Peace to her soul because she was very young. That is the only burial that I ever saw in the village. What struck and moved me was that her whole family was crying behind the stretcher where the body rested, and her husband more than anyone. In his grief he was tearing his long white traditional shirt as he walked behind his wife's body. And her mother-in-law, too, was tearing her dress. I saw the naked breasts of this elderly woman who fell facedown on the torn pieces of cloth. I had never seen despair like this. This woman they were burying was loved, her death afflicted the entire family, the whole village.

Was I actually there or did I witness the burial from the terrace? Probably from the terrace because I was too young. In any case, I was crying, too. There were many people and they moved slowly into the village. And this man who was crying out in his pain, who was ripping his shirt, I will never forget him. He was so beautiful with his cries of love for his wife. He was a man of much dignity.

My mother's parents and my uncle lived in the village. My grandfather Mounther was quite tall like his son, clean-shaven, always very well groomed and properly dressed, even if he was just wearing the traditional clothes. He always had his prayer beads in his hand and would be counting the beads with his long fingers. He came sometimes to our house to smoke his pipe with my father, and they always seemed to get along. But one day my mother left the house to spend the night at her parents' because my father had beaten her too severely. She left us alone with him. In our land, a woman may not take her children with her. Whether they are boys or girls, they stay with their father. And the older I got, the more he beat her, and the more frequently she would leave. It was my grandfather Mounther who would bring her back by force. She would leave sometimes for a week, sometimes a day, or for a night. Once she left for at least a month and my grandfather stopped speaking to my father.

I think that if my mother had died, she would never have had a burial like that woman's, and my father would not have wept or torn his shirt like Mister Hassan. He did not love my mother. I should have been convinced that love didn't exist at all in our culture, at least not in our house. Finally, I had only my brother to love despite his violence and his outbursts of madness. My sisters loved him, too. Noura had left, but Kainat was like me—she protected him and would clap her hands when he got on his horse.

Apart from the little sisters, who were too young to daydream about marriage, there were only the two of us in the house, two unmarried girls. I think Kainat was resigned to it. She wasn't homely, but still not very pretty or pleasant looking. Kainat was different from me. We were two badly dressed, unkempt peasants. But I was small and slender and she was rather robust, and her breasts were too large. The men liked the women to be a little fleshy but they didn't care for such a large bosom. She couldn't please and she didn't know how to make herself more attractive, which made her sad. Kainat grew heavy even though she ate the same thing I did, it wasn't her fault. And anyway, neither of us could make ourselves prettier than God had made us. With what? We had no beautiful dresses, always the same white or gray pants, no makeup or jewelry. And locked up like old chickens, scratching at the dirt, nose down, eyes on our feet, as soon as we set foot out of the house with our sheep.

If Kainat has no hope and closes the door to marriage for me, I at least know that a man has asked for me. My mother said to me: "Faiez's father came, he asked for you for his son. But we can't discuss marriage for the time being, we have to wait for your sister." After that, I imagined that he was waiting for me and that he was growing impatient at my parents' refusal.

My brother, Assad, knows him. Faiez lives in the house opposite ours, on the other side of the road. They aren't peasants like us; they don't work much in their garden. His parents had three sons, and Faiez is the one who still isn't married. There are no girls in the house, that's why it's surrounded not by walls but by an attractive low enclosure, and the door is never locked. The walls are pink and the car that is always parked in front is gray.

Faiez works in the city. I don't know what he does, but I suppose he is in an office, like my uncle. In any case, he is much better dressed than Hussein, my older sister's husband. Hussein is always in workmen's clothes, never very clean, and he smells bad. Faiez is all elegance, a beautiful car with four seats, which starts up every morning. I begin to spy on his car to get a look at him. The best observation spot is the terrace where I shake out the sheepskin carpets and pick grapes and set out the laundry to dry. If I pay attention I can always find something to do up there. I notice that he always parks his car in the same place, a few steps from the door. I can't stay too long at a time on the terrace, so it takes me several days of watching to discover that he leaves at about seven every morning, a time when it is rather easy for me to find something to do on the terrace.

The first time I saw him I was lucky. I cleaned the stable in a hurry, and I brought dry hay for a sick ewe that was about to give birth. I had taken two or three steps with the hay when he came out, as elegant as my uncle, in a suit, with beautiful black-and-tan laced shoes, carrying a briefcase, very black hair, very tanned complexion, a proud bearing.

I lowered my head, my nose in the straw. I heard him walk to the car, the clacking sound of the car door closing, the motor starting up, and the tires on the gravel. I raised my head only when the car was in the distance, and I waited for it to disappear, my heart beating loudly in my chest and my legs trembling. And I said to myself: *I want this man for my husband. I love him. I want him, I want him . . .*

But what to do? How could I plead with him to go and beg my father to conclude the marriage? How could I even speak to him first? A girl does not speak first to a man. She is not even supposed to look directly at him. He is inaccessible. Even if this man wants to marry me, it's not for him to decide it. It's my father, always him, and he would kill me if he knew I lingered for a second on the road with my load of hay to draw Faiez's attention.

I didn't hope for much that day but I wanted him to see me, wanted him to know that I was waiting, too. So I decided to do everything I could to meet him in secret and speak to him, at the risk of being beaten or stoned to death. I didn't want to wait any longer for Kainat to leave the house. It could take months or years, it was too unfair. I didn't want to grow older and become the mockery of the village. I didn't want to lose all hope of going away with a man, of getting free of my father's brutality.

Every morning and every evening, I will be on the terrace watching for my beloved, until he looks up at me and gives me a sign. A smile. If not, I'm certain he will ask for another girl from the village or somewhere else. And one day, I will see another woman getting into this car in my place. She will steal Faiez from me.

The Secret

I put my life at risk in telling this love story, which begins almost twenty-five years ago in my native village in the Palestinian Territory, a tiny place, then a region occupied by the Israelis. If I named it, I could be in danger, even thousands of kilometers from there. I am officially dead in my village, my existence has been forgotten for a long time, but if I were to go back today they would try to kill me a second time for the honor of my family. It's the law of the land.

On the terrace of the family house, watching for the man I love to appear, I am a young girl in mortal danger. But all I can think of is marriage. It is springtime. I couldn't say what month, probably April. In my village, we don't measure time the same way as in Europe. You never know exactly how old your father or mother is, you don't even know the date of your own birth. Time is calculated by Ramadan, by the seasons of the harvests or the gathering of figs. The sun is your guide and it marks the beginning and end of your working day.

At the time this all happened, I think I might have been about seventeen years old. I will discover later a document which claims that I am nineteen. But I don't know where this paper came from. It's very possible that my mother confused the birth of one daughter with that of another when she had to give me an official existence. I am mature from the time my periods start, eligible now for marriage for the last three or four celebrations of Ramadan. I will be a woman the day of my wedding. My own mother is still young in years but seems old already; my father looks old because he doesn't have many teeth left. Faiez is certainly older than me, but that's a good thing. I expect security from him. My brother, Assad, was married too young, to a girl his own age. If she doesn't give him sons, one day he will need another woman.

I hear Faiez's footsteps on the gravel. I shake my wool rug over the edge of the terrace. He looks up. He sees me and I know he has understood. No sign, especially not a word spoken, he gets into his car and drives off. My first rendezvous, an unforgettable emotion, has lasted the time it takes to eat an olive.

The next morning, I'm more adventurous. I pretend to be chasing a goat in order to pass in front of his house. Faiez smiles at me, and because the car doesn't start up right away, I know he's watching me go off toward the fields with the animals. The air is cooler in the morning, which gives me a chance to wear my red woolen jacket, my only new piece of clothing, which I've buttoned up to the neck, and which makes me prettier to look at. If I could dance right in the middle of the sheep I would do it. My second rendezvous has lasted longer, because when I turn my head just a little at the edge of the village, I see that he has not yet started the engine. I can't go any farther in taking the initiative. Now it's for him to decide how he will arrange to speak to me in secret. He knows where I go and when. The next day my mother isn't home, she's gone to the city with my father; my brother is with his wife, and Kainat is taking care of the stable and the little sisters. I am alone and I go out to cut grass for the rabbits. After I've walked a quarter of an hour, Faiez appears in front of me. He has followed me discreetly and says hello to me. His sudden presence stuns me. I look around me uneasily to make sure my brother isn't coming, or someone from the village. There is no one but I go toward the shelter of a high embankment at the edge of the field and Faiez follows me. I am ashamed and I look down at my feet, I twist the fabric of my dress and pull on the buttons of my jacket, I don't know what to say. He assumes an attractive pose, a stem of green wheat between his teeth, and looks me over.

"Why aren't you married?"

"I have to find the man for me, and my sister has to be married first."

"Your father has spoken to you?"

"He told me your father came to see him a long time ago."

"Are you all right at home?"

"He'll beat me if he sees me with you."

"Would you like us to get married together?"

"But my sister has to be the first."

"You're afraid?"

"Yes, I'm afraid. My father is mean. It's dangerous for you, too. My father could beat both of us."

He stays there, sits down calmly behind the embankment, while I move quickly to gather the grass. He seems to be waiting for me but he knows very well I can't go back to the village with him. I asked him to stay there a few minutes to give me a chance to return alone. And I walk quickly to get back to the house, proud of myself. I want him to have a good impression of me and think

77

of me as a good girl. I have to be careful of my reputation as far as he's concerned, because I'm the one who made the first move.

I have never been so happy. It's so wonderful to be with him, so close, even for a few minutes. I feel it in my whole body. I can't think about it clearly, I'm too naive, I'm no more educated than a goat, but this wonderful feeling is about the freedom of my heart, and my body, too. For the first time in my life I am someone because I myself decided to do what I want. I am alive. I'm not obeying my father or anyone else. On the contrary, I'm disobeying.

I have a pretty clear memory of these moments and the ones that will follow. I had almost no sense of myself before this experience. I didn't know what I looked like, whether or not I was pretty. I wasn't aware of being a human being, of thinking, of having feelings. What I have always known is fear, the suffering and humiliation of being tied up like an animal in the stable and beaten so hard I had no feeling in my back . . . the terror at the possibility of being suffocated or thrown into a well. I have received so many blows with docility. Even if my father can't run very fast anymore, he always finds a way to catch hold of us. It's easy for him to bang my head on the edge of the bathtub because I knocked over some water. It's easy for him to hit me on the legs when the tea arrives late. You can't think about yourself when you live like this. My first real meeting with Faiez, in the field of green wheat, gives me for the first time of my existence an idea of who I am. A woman, impatient to see Faiez, who loves him and who is determined to become his wife at any price.

The next day, on the same road, he waits for me to go to the field and comes to join me.

"Do you look at other boys besides me?"

"No. Never."

"Do you want me to speak to your father about the marriage?"

I would like to kiss his feet for that. I want him to go now, at this very moment, to run and announce to my father that he, Faiez, doesn't want to wait, that he must ask my family for me, bring gold for me and jewels, and prepare a great feast.

"I'll give you a sign for the next time, and don't wear your red jacket, it's too visible and that's dangerous."

The days pass, the sun rises and sets, and morning and evening I watch from the terrace for a sign from him. Now I'm certain he's in love with me. The last time we were to meet, he didn't come. I waited a long time, more than a quarter of an hour, risking being late getting home and having my father come after me. I was anxious and unhappy, but he was there the next time. From a distance, I saw him coming down the road. He signaled for me to hide at the end of the field, behind the embankment where no one can see us because the grass is so high.

"Why didn't you come?"

"I did come, but I hid farther off to see if you might be meeting someone else."

"I don't meet with anyone else."

"The boys whistle when you pass."

"I don't look at anyone. I'm a good girl."

"Now I know that. I've seen your father. We'll be married soon."

He did it, he had gone to see my father after the second meeting. And even if the date wasn't fixed, the year wouldn't end without my being married. It was warm and beautiful that day, the figs are not yet ripe but I'm sure I won't have to wait for the beginning of summer and the harvests before my mother makes ready the concoction to prepare me for my wedding night. Faiez comes closer to me, very close. I close my eyes, I'm a little afraid. I feel his hand behind my neck and he kisses me on the mouth. I immediately push him away, without saying anything, but my gesture says: *Look out. Don't go any farther.*

"See you tomorrow. Wait for me, but not on the road, it's too dangerous. Hide here, in the ditch. I'll meet you after work."

He is the first to leave. I wait for him to be far enough away before going back, as usual, but more nervously this time. This kiss, the first one of my life, has overwhelmed me. And the next day, as I watch him approach my hiding place, my heart is trembling No one in the house suspects my secret meetings.

In the mornings, my sister sometimes goes with me to take the sheep and the goats to pasture, but she usually goes back to take care of the stable and the house, and I remain alone in the afternoons. The grass is tall in spring and the sheep take advantage of it. It's thanks to them I'm able to be away by myself. It's a false freedom that my family grants me, because my father carefully watches the time of my departure and return. The village, the neighbors, they're all there to remind me about the consequences of misbehavior. I communicate with Faiez by almost invisible signals from the terrace. From a movement of the head I know he will come. But if he gets into his car without looking up, he won't be coming. That day I know he will come, he confirmed it for me. And I feel strongly that something is going to happen.

I'm afraid Faiez wants more than a kiss, and at the same time I want it without really knowing what is waiting for me. I'm afraid that if he goes too far and I push him away, he'll get angry. I also have confidence in him because he knows very well I can't let myself be touched before marriage. He knows very well that I'm not a *charmuta*. And he has promised me marriage. But I'm afraid all the same, all alone in this field with the flock. Hidden in the tall grass, I watch the animals and the road. I don't see anyone. The field is magnificent with all the flowers that are blooming. The sheep are calm in this season, they spend the time eating, not wandering off as they do in the height of summer when the grass is scarcer.

I was expecting him to come up on my right side, but he arrives from the other direction, surprising me. That's good, he's cautious about not being seen, he's protecting me. He is so handsome. He's wearing pants that are tight from the waist to the knee and wide from the knee down. It's the fashion for men who dress in the modern Western way. He has a white sweater with long sleeves and a V-neck, which exposes the hair on his chest. I find him elegant, so chic next to me. I have obeyed, I haven't worn my red jacket, so I can't be seen from a distance. My dress is gray, and also my pants. I washed my clothes carefully because with the work they're often dirty. I've concealed my hair beneath a white scarf, but I miss my beautiful red jacket, I would have liked to be so much prettier.

We sit on the ground, he kisses me. He tries to place his hand on my thigh. I don't let him do it. He gets annoyed. His expression is mean as he looks at me.

"Why don't you want to? Come on!"

I'm so afraid he'll go away, that he'll look for somebody else. He can do that whenever he wants, he's a good-looking man, my future husband. I love him, I wouldn't want to give in, I'm too afraid, but even more afraid of losing him. He is my only hope. So I let him do what he wants without knowing what is going to happen to me, and how far he'll go. He is there, before my eyes, he wants to touch me, nothing else matters. The sun will be setting soon, it's less hot, I don't have much time left before I have to take the sheep back. He pushes me into the grass, and he does what he wants. I say nothing more, I don't resist. He isn't violent, he doesn't force me, he knows very well what he's doing. The pain takes me by surprise. I wasn't expecting it, but that's not why I'm crying. He says nothing, either before or after, he doesn't ask me why I'm crying, and I don't even know why I have so many tears. I wouldn't know what to say to him even if he asked. I didn't want to. I'm a virgin, I know nothing about love between a man and a woman, no one has taught me anything about it. The woman is supposed to bleed, with her husband, that's all I've learned since my childhood. He does what he wants in silence, until I bleed, and all of a sudden he looks surprised, as if he didn't expect that. Did he believe that I had already done this with other men? Because I was alone with my sheep? He himself said that he had watched me and saw I was an honest girl. I don't dare look at him, I'm ashamed. He raises my chin and he says: "I love you."

"I love you, too."

I didn't understand at the moment that he was proud of himself. It was only much later that I felt the anger that he had doubted my honor, that he had used me when he knew how much I was risking. I didn't want to make love with him hidden in a ditch, I wanted what all the girls of my village want. To be married, to have the ritual hair removal, to have a beautiful dress and go to bed in his house. I wanted him to show everyone at sunrise the white linen with the red stain. I wanted to hear the women's ululations. He took advantage of my fear, he knew I would give in to keep him.

I ran to hide nearby, to wipe the blood off my legs and straighten my clothes while he calmly put himself in order. Afterward, I begged him not to drop me, to arrange the marriage quickly. A girl who is no longer a virgin, this is too serious, it's all over for her.

"I'll never drop you."

"I love you."

"I love you, too. Now go back, change your clothes, and act like nothing happened. Especially don't cry in the house."

He left ahead of me. I'd stopped crying but I felt a little sick. This blood was disgusting. Making love with a man wasn't a celebration. I felt bad, I felt dirty, I had no water to wash myself, nothing but the grass to wipe myself with. I still felt the burning in my belly, and I had to collect the sheep, and return home, with my dirty pants. I'd have to do the washing in secret. As I hurried back, I thought I probably wouldn't bleed anymore but wondered if I would always feel so bad with my husband. Would it always be so disgusting?

Is my expression normal when I reach the house? I'm not crying anymore but I hurt inside and I'm afraid. I realize what I have done. I'm not a virgin anymore. I'm no longer safe as long as I'm not married. I won't be a virgin on my wedding night. But that's not important because he knows I was a virgin with him. I'll arrange it somehow, I'll cut myself with a knife, I'll stain the marriage linen with my blood. I will be like all the other women.

I wait for three days. I watch from the terrace for Faiez to give me a signal for a meeting. This time, he leads me into a little shelter of stones, at the other end of the field. It's a place where we'd be out of the rain. This time I don't bleed. I still have discomfort but much less fear. All I care about is that he come back. He is there and I love him even more. What he does with my body isn't important, it's in my head that I love him. He is my whole life, all my hope of leaving my parents' house, of being a woman who walks with a man in the street, who gets into a car with him to do the shopping and goes to stores to buy dresses and shoes. I am happy to be with him, to belong to him. He's a man, a real one, a capable man. I am confident about the marriage. He doesn't know when, and neither do I, but I don't ask any questions. In my mind, it is certain.

Until it happens, I must be watchful that I'm not denounced by someone. For the next meeting, I'll change my route. I figure the extra time I'll need, and in the meantime I don't dare leave the house by myself by the iron door. I wait to be with my mother or my sister. I watch for Faiez to leave every morning. As soon as I hear his steps on the gravel, I go quickly to the cement wall. If someone else is outside I turn my back; if there is no one I wait for the signal. Two more rendezvous since the first one when I lost my virginity. We can't see each other every day, it wouldn't be wise. It's another six days before he gives the signal for the third meeting. I'm still afraid, and still confident. I pay attention to the slightest noise in the countryside. I avoid waiting at the side of the road. I wait in the grass in a ditch, with my stick. I watch the bees in the wildflowers, and I dream about the day soon to come when I won't be guarding sheep and goats anymore, when I won't be cleaning out the manure in the stable. He is going to come, he loves me, and when he leaves again I will say to him, like the first and the second times: *Don't abandon me.*

We make love for the third time. The sun is yellow, I must milk the sheep and the cows. I say: "I love you, don't abandon me. When will you come back?"

"We can't see each other right away. We'll wait a little. We have to be careful."

"For how long?"

"Until I give you a sign."

My love affair had gone on for two weeks, three meetings in the field with the sheep. Faiez is right to be careful, and I must be patient, wait for my parents to speak to me, as they spoke to my sister Noura. My father can't still be waiting to marry Kainat before me! Since Faiez has asked for me and she is still unmarried at twenty, he can get me off his hands. He still has two more daughters! Khadija and Salima, the little ones, will be put to work in their turn with my mother and will take over the flocks and the harvesting. Fatma, my brother's wife, is pregnant again, she's supposed to give birth soon. She can work, too. I await my destiny. Always with a little fear. The days pass and Faiez gives me no sign. I'm hopeful all the same, every evening, of seeing him appear out of nowhere, as he can do, to the left or right of the ravine where I hide.

One morning in the stable I suddenly feel very strange. The odor of the manure makes me dizzy. And later as I prepare the meal, the mutton makes me feel ill. I'm nervous, I want to go to sleep or cry for no reason. Every time Faiez comes out of his house he looks somewhere else, makes no sign to me. It's been a long time, too long, and I don't know when I last had my period, or when it should arrive. I often heard my mother ask my sister Noura: "You have your periods?"

"Yes, Mama."

And, too: "You haven't had your period? That's good, it means you're pregnant!"

I don't see mine coming. I check several times a day. Every time I go to the bathroom, I look to see if there's any blood. Sometimes I feel so strange that I think it must have come. But there's still no blood. And I'm so afraid that the fear grips my throat as if

I were going to vomit. I don't feel the way I did before, I don't want to work, to get up. My nature has changed. I try to find a reason that isn't the worst one. I ask myself if the shock of not being a virgin anymore can change a girl this way. Maybe the periods don't come back right away. I can't of course get any information about this naive explanation. The least question on this subject would cause thunderbolts to come down on me. I think about it constantly, every moment of the day and especially at night when I fall asleep near my sisters. If I'm pregnant my father is going to smother me in the sheepskin blanket. In the morning when I get up I'm happy just to be alive.

I'm afraid someone in the family is going to notice that I'm not normal. I want to vomit in front of the plate of sugared rice, I want to go to sleep in the stable. I feel tired, my cheeks are pale, my mother is certainly going to notice this and ask me if I'm sick. So I hide, I pretend to be fine, but it becomes more and more difficult. And still Faiez doesn't appear. He gets into his car wearing his beautiful suit, with his briefcase and his fine shoes, and he takes off so fast that his car makes a cloud of dust. Summer begins. It gets very hot in the morning. I am supposed to take the animals out at dawn and bring them back before the sun is too strong. I can't be on the terrace anymore watching for him, although I absolutely must speak to him about the marriage. Because a strange spot has appeared on my nose. A small brown spot that I try to hide because I know what it means. Noura had the same thing when she was pregnant. My mother looked at me with surprise: "What did you do to yourself?"

"It's henna, it was on my hands and I rubbed my nose, I wasn't paying attention."

I really did put on henna and purposely smudged my nose. But this lie can't go on for long. I am pregnant and it's been a month since the last time I saw Faiez.

I must speak to him. One evening, when the sun is not yet down, I boil water in the garden to do the wash so that I can go up onto the terrace with my laundry at about the time when I know he's going to come home. This time, I give him a signal with my head and I keep gesturing to make him understand: *I want to see you, I'm going down there, you must follow me . . .*

He has seen me and I run off to wait for him, pretending to go watch over a sick sheep in the stable. The sheep is really sick, we're waiting for her to give birth, and it's not the first time I've stayed near her. I've even slept on the straw a whole night for fear of not hearing her.

He arrives at our rendezvous spot a little after me, and he immediately tries to make love, convinced that's why I called him. I draw back.

"No, that's not why I wanted to see you."

"Well, why then?"

"I want to talk to you."

"We'll talk after. Come on!"

"You don't love me. Can't we meet just to talk?"

"Yes, but I love you, I love you so much that every time I see you I want you."

"Faiez, the first time I wanted nothing, then you kissed me, and I accepted three times, now I haven't had my period."

"Maybe it's just late?"

"No, I've never been late and I feel strange."

He doesn't want to make love anymore. His face has gone blank.

"What are we going to do?"

"We have to get married, now! We can't wait, you have to go see my father, even if there isn't any wedding, I don't care!"

"They'll talk in the village, it's not done! What would we do about putting out the sheet on the balcony?"

"Don't worry about that, I'll take care of it."

"But we can't have a small ceremony, we said a big wedding, we'll have a big wedding. I'll go talk to your father. Wait for me here tomorrow at the same time."

"But it's not always possible for me. You're a man, you do what you want. Wait for me to give you a sign. If I can, you'll see me braiding my hair. If I don't take off my scarf, don't come."

The next day, I take a chance saying I'm going to gather some grass for the sick sheep. I give the signal and I run to the meeting place, trembling. My father has said nothing, I've heard nothing. I'm so afraid that I can't get my breath. Faiez arrives a good half hour after me. I attack him.

"Why haven't you gone to see my father?"

"I don't dare look your father in the face. I'm afraid."

"But you have to hurry, it's been almost two months now. My stomach is going to start getting big. What am I going to do?" And I start to cry.

"Stop it, don't be crying when you go home. I'm going to see your father tomorrow."

I believed him, I wanted so much to believe him. Because I loved him and I had good reason to hope, because he had already asked my father for me once. I understood that he was afraid to face him. It wasn't easy to explain why he wanted the marriage to take place so soon. What reason could he find in the face of my father's mistrust and meanness, without revealing the secret and destroying my honor and his own before the family?

I prayed to God that night, as usual. My parents were very religious, my mother went often to the mosque. The girls were supposed to say their prayers twice a day in the house. The next day when I woke up I thanked Allah that I was alive.

The car had already left when I went out to the terrace. Then I did my work as usual, I cared for the sheep, cleaned the stable, I brought out the flock, picked the tomatoes. I waited for evening. I was so afraid that I picked up a big stone and struck my stomach with it hoping to make myself bleed and put things right.

The Last Meeting

Evening has come. I am desperate for Faiez to arrive, alone or with his parents, but I know very well that he won't. It's too late for today. And the car isn't parked in front of his house, the shutters have remained closed. This is dreadful for me. I spend the night awake, trying to make myself believe that he went to see his family somewhere; that if the shutters are closed it's because of the heat.

It is extraordinary how these few weeks of my life have stayed imprinted on my memory. I who have so much difficulty reconstructing my childhood, except for the images of cruelty, the absence of happiness and peace, I have never forgotten these moments of stolen freedom, of fear and hope. I can see myself so clearly that night under my sheepskin cover, my knees up under my chin, holding my stomach with my two hands, listening for the least sound in the dark. *Tomorrow he'll be there . . . Tomorrow he won't be there . . . He's going to rescue me, he's going to abandon me . . .* It was like music playing in my head that wouldn't stop.

The next morning, I see the car in front of the house. I say to myself: *He's alive!* There is hope. I can't go to watch for him to leave, but in the evening when he returns I'm out on the terrace. I signal for a meeting the next day before sunset. And at the end of the afternoon, just before sunset, I go to fetch hay for the sheep. I wait ten minutes, a quarter of an hour, hoping that perhaps he's hidden a little farther off. The harvest is over but in certain places of the field I can collect some good sheaves, which I tie up with straw. I line them up near the path and knot them first. I work quickly but I am careful to leave three sheaves untied in case somebody passes by because I'm very visible in this spot. I'd only have to bend over my sheaves and look very busy at my work, which I've already finished. That gives me a quarter of an hour extra before I have to go back to the house. I told my mother I'd return with the hay in a half hour. At this time of day, the sheep have already been brought in, the goats and the cows, too, and I still have to milk them for the next day's cheeses. I've employed almost every pretext for this rendezvous. I went to the well to draw water for the animals, which requires three short trips with a big bucket balanced on my head. The rabbits needed tender grass, the chickens needed grain that I went to collect. I wanted to see if the figs were beginning to ripen, I needed lemon for the cooking, I had to relight the fire in the bread oven.

I must always be mistrustful of my parents, who are mistrustful of their daughter. A daughter may do many things. Is she going into the courtyard? What is she doing there? She hasn't by chance arranged a tryst behind the bread oven? She's going to the well? Did she take the bucket with her? Haven't the animals already been watered? She's going for hay? How many sheaves does she bring back?

That evening, I drag my cloth sack from sheaf to sheaf. I fill it quickly and I wait, and wait. I know that my father is sitting as usual under the lamp in front of the house, smoking his pipe like a pasha and waiting with his belt for the daughter to return at the time she's supposed to return. He's counting the minutes. He has a watch. If I've said a half hour, that's a half hour minus one minute if I don't want to get a whipping with the belt.

I have just three sheaves to tie up. The sky is turning gray, the yellow of the sun is growing paler. I don't have a watch but I know I have only a few minutes left before night falls, which happens suddenly in my country. It's as though the sun is so tired of giving us light that it falls like a stone, leaving us abruptly in the dark.

I have lost hope. It's over. He's dropped me. I arrive home. His car isn't there. I get up the next morning, his car is still not there. It's really the end. There's no more hope of going on living. And I have understood. He took advantage of me, it was a fine time for him. Not for me. I tear at my hair but it's too late. I'll never see him again. At the end of the week, I've even stopped watching for him from the terrace. The shutters of the pink house are closed, he has fled in his car like a coward. I can't ask anyone for help.

At three or four months, my stomach begins to get larger. I can still conceal it pretty well under my dress but as soon as I carry a bucket or any load on my head, with my back arched and arms raised, I have to make a considerable effort to hide it. And the spot on my nose, I try to rub it off, but it doesn't go away. I can't try the henna again, my mother wouldn't believe me.

My anguish is strongest at night. I often go out to sleep with the sheep. The pretext is ready-made: When a sheep is about to give birth, she calls out like a human, and if help isn't at hand the little one can suffocate in the mother's womb. I sometimes think about this particular sheep, whose baby was having trouble getting out. I had to put my arm all the way into her, very gently, to turn the lamb's head in a better direction and pull it toward me. I was afraid of hurting it, and I struggled a long time to retrieve this little lamb. The mother wasn't able to push, the poor thing, and I had to give her a lot of help. And an hour later she died.

The lamb was a little female. She would follow me about like a child. As soon as she would see me leave, she would call to me. I would milk the other sheep first and then feed her with a bottle. I helped many sheep give birth but this is the only one I remember. The little one followed me in the garden, she went up the stairs of the house. She was behind me everywhere I went. The mother was dead and the lamb was alive . . .

It's strange to think that we would make such an effort helping a sheep give birth when my mother was suffocating her children. At the time I certainly didn't think about it. It was a custom that you had to accept. In letting these images play out in my memory today, I am revolted. If I'd had the awareness that I have today, I would have strangled my mother to save even one of those little girls.

What can my father do to me if he finds out that I'm pregnant? My sister Kainat and I thought that being tied up in the stable was the worst thing that could happen to us, our hands tied behind our backs, a scarf stuffed into our mouths so we wouldn't yell, and our feet bound with the rope he used for beating us. Mute, awake all night, we would just look at each other, thinking the same thing: *As long as we're tied up we're still alive.*

And so it's my father who comes toward me, on a washing day.

I hear him coming up behind me, his cane striking the ground of the courtyard. He stops behind me. I don't dare get up.

"I'm sure you're pregnant."

I drop the laundry into the basin, I haven't the strength to look up at him. I can't let myself appear surprised or humiliated. And I won't be able to lie if I look at him.

"No, Papa."

"Oh yes! Look at yourself! You've gotten big. And that spot there, you say it's from the sun, then you say it's henna? Your mother has to see your breasts."

So it's my mother who suspected. And he's the one who gives the order.

"You have to show them."

And my father goes off with his cane without another word. He hasn't struck me. I didn't protest, my mouth is paralyzed. I think this time this is it, I'm dead. It's now my mother's turn. She is calm but rough.

"Now leave the laundry alone! Show me your breasts!"

"No, please Mama, that bothers me."

"You show them to me or I'll rip your dress!"

So I undo the buttons of my collar down to my chest and move the cloth apart.

"You're pregnant?"

"No!"

"You've had your period?"

"Yes!"

"The next time you have your period you'll show me!"

I said yes, to remain calm, to calm her down, and for my safety. I know I'm going to have to cut myself and smear the blood on a piece of paper and show it to her at the next full moon.

I leave off the washing and go out of the house without permission and I climb up and hide in the branches of an old lemon tree. It's stupid to seek out this shelter, the lemon tree isn't going to save me, but I'm so afraid I don't know what I'm doing. Very soon my father comes to look for me and he finds me there, in the branches. He only has to tug on my legs to make me fall. One of my knees is bleeding. He leads me back to the house, and he takes some sage leaves and chews them and applies this pulp to the wound to stop the bleeding. This is strange. I don't understand why after making me fall so roughly, now he goes to the trouble of taking care of me, which he has never done. I thought maybe he isn't really mean after all, he believed what I told him. With the distance of time, I think it was just to prevent me from using this blood to make them believe that I'd had my period. I had a pain in my stomach when I fell and I hope the fall will make it come.

A little later, there is a family meeting, which I'm not allowed to attend. My parents have had Noura and Hussein come. I'm listening behind the wall. They're all talking and I hear my father say: "I'm sure she's pregnant. She doesn't want to tell us. We're waiting for her to show us her period . . ."

As soon as they stop talking, I go upstairs and pretend to be sleeping. The next day my parents go to the city. I'm forbidden to go out. The courtyard door is closed but I go through the garden and I run and hide in the fields. I start to hit my stomach with a big stone, through my dress, to make the blood come. No one ever explained to me how a baby grows in its mother's stomach. I know that at a certain moment the baby moves. I have seen my mother pregnant, I know how much time it takes for the baby to come into the world, but I'm ignorant of all the rest. From what moment is the baby alive? For me, it's at the moment of birth, since that's when I saw my mother make the choice of letting them live or die. What I ardently hope for, although I've been pregnant for three or four months, is that the blood will come back. That's all I think about. I don't even imagine that this child in my belly is already a human being. And I weep with rage and fear because the stone I'm hitting myself with doesn't make the blood come. Because my parents are going to return and I must get back to the house ahead of them.

This memory is so painful now, I feel so guilty. It's no good telling myself that I was ignorant, terrified of what awaited me. It is a nightmare to think that I hammered like this on my stomach for this child not to exist.

And the next day, it's the same thing, I strike my stomach with anything I can find, and at every opportunity. My mother is waiting for me. She has given me a month from the day when she made me show her my breasts. I know she's counting in her head, and while she waits I'm not allowed to go out. I have to remain confined to the house and keep to household chores. My mother has said to me: "You don't go out that door again! You're not to watch the sheep, you're not to go out to fetch the hay." I can escape through the courtyard and the gardens but to go where? I have never taken the bus alone, I don't have any money, and anyway the driver wouldn't let me on. I must be in the fifth month. I've felt movement in my belly. Like a crazy person, I press my stomach against the wall. But I can't get away with lying anymore or trying to conceal my stomach and my breasts. There is no way out.

The only idea that occurs to me, the only possible one, is to flee from the house and ask my mother's sister to take me in.

She lives in the village, I know her house. So one morning, while my parents are out at the market, I cross the garden, I pass by the well, I jump over the embankment, and I make my way to her house. I don't have much hope because she is mean, jealous of my mother for reasons I don't know about. But just maybe she'll keep me and find a solution. Seeing me arrive alone, she expresses concern about my parents. Why haven't they come with me?

"You have to help me, Aunt."

And I tell her everything, the hoped-for marriage that hasn't happened, the wheat field.

"Who is it?"

"His name is Faiez, but he's not here anymore, he promised . . ."

"All right. I'm going to help you."

She dresses, puts on her scarf, and takes me by the hand.

"Come, we're going to take a walk together."

"But where? What are you going to do?"

"Come, give me your hand, you can't be seen walking alone."

I suppose she's going to take me to another woman, a neighbor who has secrets for making a girl's period start or keeping the child from continuing to grow in my belly. Or she's going to hide me someplace until I'm freed.

But she takes me home. She pulls me like a donkey who doesn't want to move.

"Why are you taking me home? Help me, I beg you!"

"Because that's your place, it's for them to take care of you, not me."

"I beg you, stay with me! You know what's going to happen to me!"

"This is where you belong! You understand? And don't go out again!"

She forces me to go through the door, calls to my parents, turns around and leaves. I saw the meanness, the scorn in her expression. She must have thought: *My sister has a serpent in her house, this girl has dishonored her family.*

My father closes the door and my mother glowers at me and makes a gesture with her chin and hand that means: *Charmuta . . . slut . . . you dared to go to my sister!* They despise each other. A misfortune happens to one and the other is gleeful.

"Yes, I went to her, I thought she could help me, hide me . . ."

"Go upstairs!"

My whole body is trembling, my legs won't support me. I don't know what will happen to me once I'm locked up in the room. I can't make myself move.

"Souad! Get up there!"

My sister has stopped speaking to me. She is as ashamed as I am and she doesn't leave the house anymore. My mother works as usual, my other sisters take care of the animals, and they leave me locked up like someone with a contagious disease. I hear them talking together now and then. They're afraid that someone may have seen me in the village, that people have started talking. In trying to save myself by going to my aunt, I have especially shamed my mother. The neighbors will know, the tongues will be wagging, the ears will be listening.

From that day on, I can't put my nose outside. My father has installed a new lock on the door of the room where I sleep and it makes a sound like a gunshot every night when he secures it. The garden door makes the same sound. Sometimes when I'm doing the washing in the courtyard, I feel suffocated when I look at that door. I'll never leave here. I don't even realize that this door is stupid because the garden and the embankment of stones that protects it are not objects that can't be crossed or climbed over. I've gone out that way more than once. But the prison is secure for any girl in my situation. It would be worse outside. Outside there is shame, scorn, stones thrown, neighbors who would spit in my face or drag me home by my hair. I don't even dream about the outside. And the weeks pass. No one questions me, no one wants to know who did this to me, how and why. Even if I accuse Faiez, my father won't go looking for him to make him marry me. It's my fault, not his. A man who has taken a girl's virginity is not guilty, she was willing. And even worse she's the one who asked for it, who provoked the man because she is a whore without honor. I have no defense. My naïveté, my love for him, his promise of marriage, even his first request to my father, nothing of all that counts for anything. In our culture, a man who has self-respect doesn't marry the girl he has deflowered.

Did he love me? No. And if I committed a fault, it was believing that I would hold on to him by doing what he wanted. Was I in love? Was I afraid he would find somebody else? That is not a defense, and even to me it had stopped making sense.

One evening, another family meeting: my parents, my older sister, and her husband, Hussein. My brother isn't there because his wife is about to give birth and he's gone to be with her and her family. I listen behind the wall, terrified.

My mother speaks to Hussein: "We can't ask our son, he won't be able to do it, he's too young."

"I can take care of her."

Then my father speaks: "If you're going to do it, it must be done right. What do you have in mind?"

"Don't worry about it. I'll find a way."

My mother again: "You'll have to take care of her, but you'll have to do it quickly."

I hear my sister crying, saying she doesn't want to hear this and that she wants to go home. Hussein tells her to wait and adds, for my parents: "You'll go out. Leave the house, you can't be there. When you come back, it will be done."

I had heard my death sentence with my own ears and I slipped back up the stairs because my sister was about to leave. I didn't hear the rest of it. A little later my father made the tour of the house and the door of the girls' room clanged shut. I didn't sleep. I couldn't comprehend what I had heard. I wondered if it could have been a dream, a nightmare? Are they really going to do it? Is it just to frighten me? And if they do it, when will it be? How? By cutting off my head? Maybe they're going to let me have this child and then kill me after? Will they keep the child if it's a boy? Will my mother suffocate it if it's a girl? Are they going to kill me first?

The next day, I act as though I've heard nothing. I am on my guard but I don't really believe it. And then I start trembling again, and I do believe it. The only questions are when and where. It can't happen immediately because Hussein has left. And then I can't imagine Hussein wanting to kill me!

My mother says to me that day, with the same tone as always: "It's time for you to do the washing, your father and I are going to the city."

I know what is going to happen. They are leaving the house just as they'd told Hussein.

Recently, when I remembered the disappearance of my sister Hanan, I realized that it happened the same way. The parents were out, the girls were alone in the house with their brother. The only difference in my case is that Hussein was not there yet. I looked at the courtyard: It was a big space, part of it was tiled, the rest covered in sand. It was encircled by a wall, and all around on top of the wall were iron spikes. And in one corner, the gray metallic door, smooth on the courtyard side, without a lock or key, with a handle only on the outside.

My sister Kainat never does the laundry with me, it doesn't take two of us. I don't know what work they've told her to do, or where she is with the little ones. She's stopped speaking to me. She sleeps with her back to me ever since I tried to escape to my aunt. My mother is waiting for me to gather the laundry. There is a lot of it because we usually do the laundry only once a week. If I begin around two or three o'clock in the afternoon, I won't be finished before six o'clock in the evening.

I first go for water from the well, at the back of the garden. I arrange the wood for the fire, I place the big laundry tub on it, and I half fill it. I sit down on a stone while I wait for the water to heat. My parents leave by the main door of the house, which they always lock on their way out.

I'm on the other side, in this courtyard. I keep the coals going all the time. The fire should not be allowed to burn down because the water has to be very hot before the laundry is put in. Then I'll rub the stains with olive oil soap, and I'll go back to the well for the rinse water. It is long and tiring work that I've been doing for years, but at this moment it's particularly painful.

I'm sitting on a rock, barefoot, in a dress of gray cloth, tired of being afraid. I don't even know anymore how long I've been pregnant with this fear in my belly. More than six months in any case. From time to time, I look over at the door in the back of the courtyard. It fascinates me. If he comes, he can only enter by that door.

The Fire

Suddenly I hear the door clang. He's there, he's coming toward me.

I see these images again twenty-five years later as if time had stopped. They are the last images of my existence in that place, in my village of the Palestinian Territory. They play out in slow motion like films on television. They come back before my eyes constantly. I'd like to erase them as soon as the first one appears but I can't stop the film from playing. When the door clangs, it's too late to stop it, I need to see it all again, these images, because I'm always trying to understand what I did not understand then. How did he do it? Could I have gotten away from him if I had understood?

He comes toward me. It's my brother-in-law Hussein in his work clothes, old pants and a T-shirt. He stands in front of me now and says, with a smile: "Hi. How goes it?" He's chewing on a blade of grass, smiling: "I'm going to take care of you."

That smile, and he says he's going to take care of me, I wasn't expecting that. I smile a little myself, to thank him, not daring to speak.

"You've got a big belly, huh?"

I lower my head, I'm ashamed to look at him. I lower my head even farther, my forehead on my knees.

"You've got a spot there. Did you put some henna there on purpose?"

"No, I put the henna on my hair, I didn't do it on purpose."

"You did it on purpose to hide it."

I look at the laundry that I was rinsing in my trembling hands. This is the last fixed and lucid image that I have: this laundry and my two trembling hands. The last words that I heard from him are: *You did it on purpose to hide it.*

He didn't say anything more. I kept my head down in shame, a little relieved that he didn't ask me other questions.

I suddenly felt a cold liquid running over my head and instantly I was on fire. It is like a movie that has been speeded up, images racing past. I start to run in the garden, barefoot. I slap my hair, I scream. I feel my dress billow out behind me. Was my dress on fire, too?

I smell the gasoline and I run, the hem of my long dress getting in the way. My terror leads me instinctively away from the courtyard. I run toward the garden as the only way out. I know I'm running and I'm on fire and I'm screaming. But I remember almost nothing after that. How did I get away? Did he run after me? Was he waiting for me to fall so he could watch me go up in flames?

I must have climbed onto the garden wall to end up then in the neighbor's garden or in the street. There were women, it seems to me two of them, so it must have been in the street, and they beat on me, I suppose with their scarves. They dragged me to the village fountain and the water hit me suddenly and I screamed in fear. I hear these women shouting but I see nothing more. My head is down against my chest. I feel the cold water running on me and I cry with pain because the water burns me. I am curled up, I smell the odor of grilled meat, the smoke. I must have fainted. I don't see much of anything after that. There are a few other vague images, sounds, as if I were in my father's van. But it's not my father. I hear the voices of women wailing over me. "The poor thing . . . The poor thing . . ." They console me. I am lying in a car. I feel the jolts of the car on the road. I hear myself moan.

And then nothing, and then again this noise of the car and the women's voices. I'm burning as if I am still on fire. I can't raise my head, I can't move my body or my arms, I am on fire, still on fire. I stink of gasoline, I don't understand anything about this sound of the car engine, the women's lamentations, I don't know where they're taking me. If I open my eyes a little, I see only a piece of my dress or my skin. It's dark, it smells. I'm still burning but the fire is out. But I'm burning all the same. In my mind I'm still running with fire all over me.

I'm going to die. That's good. Maybe I'm already dead. It's over, finally.

Dying

I am on a hospital bed, curled up in a ball under a sheet. A nurse has come to tear off my dress. She pulls roughly on the fabric, and the pain jolts me. I can see almost nothing, my chin is stuck to my chest, I can't raise it. I can't move my arms, either. The pain is in my head, on my shoulders, in my back, on my chest. I feel sick. This nurse is so mean that she frightens me when I see her come in. She doesn't speak to me. She comes to tear off pieces of me, she puts on a compress, and she goes away. If she could make me die, she would do it, I'm sure. I'm a dirty girl, if I was burned it's because I deserved it since I'm not married and I'm pregnant. I know very well what she's thinking.

Blackness. Coma. How much time passes, days or nights? No one comes to touch me, they don't look after me, they give me nothing to eat or drink, they are waiting for me to die. And I would like to die, I am so ashamed of being still alive. I'm suffering so much. I can't move. This mean woman turns me over to tear off pieces of skin. Nothing more. I would like some oil on my skin to calm the burning, I would like them to raise the sheet so the air would cool me a little. A doctor is there. I saw pant legs and a white shirt. He spoke but I didn't understand. It's always the mean woman who comes and goes. I can move my legs and I use them to raise the sheet from time to time. I'm in pain on my back, on my side. I sleep, my head still stuck to my chest, down the way it was when the fire was on me. My arms are strange, extended out away from my body and both of them paralyzed. My hands are still there, but I can't use them. I would so much like to scratch myself, to rip my skin to stop the pain.

They make me get up. I walk with this nurse. My eyes hurt. I see my legs, my hands hanging on either side of me, the tiled floor. I hate this woman. She brings me into a room and takes a shower spray to wash me. She says I smell so bad it makes her want to vomit. I stink, I weep, I am there like some dirty rotting refuse on which you'd throw a bucket of water. Like the turd in the toilet, you flush and it's gone. Die. The water tears off my skin, I scream, I weep, I beg, the blood runs down my fingers. She makes me remain standing. Under the stream of cold water she pulls off pieces of blackened skin, the shreds of my burned dress, stinking filth, which form a little pile in the bottom of the shower. I smell so strongly of rotting burned flesh and smoke that she has put on a mask and from time to time leaves the washing room, coughing and cursing me. I disgust her, I ought to die like a dog, but far away from her. Why doesn't she just finish me off? I return to my bed, burning and icy at the same time, and she throws the sheet over me so she doesn't have to look at me. *Die*, her expression says to me. *Die and let them come and pitch you somewhere else.*

My father is there with his cane. He is furious, he raps on the ground, he wants to know who made me pregnant, who brought me here, how it happened. His eyes are red. The old man is crying, but he still frightens me with that cane and I'm not even able to answer him. I'm going to go to sleep, or die, or wake up, my father was there, he isn't there anymore. But I haven't been dreaming. His voice is still ringing in my head: "Speak!"

My head is supported by a pillow and I succeed in sitting up a little so as not to feel my arms stuck to the sheet. Nothing gives me any relief but I can at least see who passes by in the corridor, since the door is half open. I hear someone, I see two bare feet, a long black dress, a small form like mine, thin, almost skinny. It's not the nurse. It's my mother.

Her two braids smoothed with olive oil, her black scarf, that strange forehead, a bulge between her eyebrows over the nose, a profile like a bird of prey. She frightens me. She sits down on a stool with her black market bag and she starts to weep, to snuffle, wiping her tears with a handkerchief, her head rocking back and forth. She weeps with unhappiness and shame. She weeps for herself and the whole family. And I see the hatred in her eyes.

She questions me, her bag clutched against her. I know this bag, it's familiar to me. She always carries it with her when she goes to the market or to the fields. She carries bread in it, a plastic bottle of water, sometimes milk. I'm afraid, but less than in my father's presence. My father can kill me, but not her. She moans her words, and I whisper.

"Look at me, my daughter. I could never bring you home like that, you can't live in the house anymore. Have you seen yourself?"

"I haven't been able to look."

"You are burned. The shame is on the whole family. I can't bring you back. Tell me how you got pregnant? Who with?"

"Faiez. I don't know his father's name."

"Faiez, the neighbor?"

She starts crying again and jabbing at her eyes with the hand-kerchief, which is rolled up in a ball, as if she wants to force it into her head.

"Where did you do it? Where?"

"In the field."

She makes a face, she bites her lip and cries even more.

"Listen to me, my child, I hope for you to die, it's better if you die. Your brother is young, if you don't die, he'll have problems."

My brother is going to have problems? What sort of problems? I don't understand.

"The police came to see the family at the house. The whole family, your father and your brother, and me, and your brother-in-law, the whole family. If you don't die, your brother will have trouble with the police."

Perhaps she took the glass out of her purse, because there is no table near the bed. No, I didn't see her look in her bag, she took it from the windowsill, it's a glass from the hospital. But I didn't see what she filled it with.

"If you don't drink this, your brother is going to have problems. The police came to the house."

Did she fill it while I was weeping with shame, with pain, with fear? I was crying about a lot of things, my head down and my eyes closed.

"Drink this . . . It's me who gives it to you."

Never will I forget this big glass, full to the top, with a trans-parent liquid, like water.

"You'll drink this, your brother won't have any problems. It's better, it's better for you, it's better for me, it's better for your brother."

And she was crying, and so was I. I remember that the tears ran down over the burns on my chin, along my neck, and they stung my skin. I couldn't raise my arms. She put a hand under my head and she raised me to the glass she was holding in her other hand. No one had given me anything to drink until then. She was bringing this big glass to my mouth. I would have liked at least to dip my lips into it, I was so thirsty. I tried to raise my chin, but I couldn't. Suddenly the doctor came into the room, and my mother jumped. He grabbed the glass from her hand and banged it down on the windowsill and he shouted: "No!" I saw the liquid run down the glass and spill over the windowsill, transparent, as clear as water. The doctor took my mother by the arm and made her leave the room. I was still looking at that glass, and I would have drunk it, I would have lapped it up like a dog. I was thirsty, as much as for water as for dying.

The doctor came back and said to me: "You're lucky I came in when I did. Your father, and now your mother! No one from your family will be allowed in here!"

"My brother, Assad, I'd like to see him, he is good."

I don't know what he answered. I felt so strange, my head was spinning. My mother had talked about the police, about my brother who supposedly had enemies? Why him, since it was Hussein who had set fire to me? That glass, it was to make me die. There was still a wet spot on the windowsill. My mother wanted me to drink it and die, and so did I. But I was lucky, according to the doctor, because I had been about to drink this invisible poison. I felt I had been delivered, as if death had tried to charm me and the doctor had made it disappear in a second. My mother was an excellent mother, the best of mothers, she was doing her duty in giving me death. It was better for me. I shouldn't have been saved

113

from the fire, brought here to suffer, and now take such a long time to die to deliver me from my shame and my family's.

My brother came, three or four days later. I will never forget that transparent plastic sack he brought. I could see oranges and a banana. I hadn't eaten or drunk anything since I'd arrived there. I wasn't able to, and anyway no one tried to help me. Even the doctor didn't dare. I knew they were letting me die, because it was forbidden to intervene in a case like mine. I was guilty in everyone's eyes. I endured the fate of all women who sully the honor of men. They had only washed me because I stank, not to provide me care. They kept me there because it was a hospital where I was supposed to die without creating other problems for my parents and the whole village. Hussein had botched the job, he had let me run away in flames.

Assad didn't ask any questions. He was afraid and he was in a hurry to get back to the village.

"I'm going to go through the fields so no one sees me. If the parents know I've come here to see you I'm going to have problems."

I had wanted him to come but I was uneasy having him lean over me. I saw in his eyes that I disgusted him with my burns. No one, not even he, was interested in how much I was suffering in this cracking, decaying, oozing skin, slowly devouring me like a serpent's venom over my whole upper body, my hairless head, my shoulders, my back, my arms, my breasts. I cried a lot. Was it because I knew it was the last time I would see him? Did I cry because I so much wanted to see his children? They were waiting for his wife to give birth, and I learned later that she had two boys. The whole family must have admired and congratulated her.

I couldn't eat the fruit. It was impossible alone and then the sack disappeared. I never saw any of my family again. My last vision of my parents is of my mother with the glass of poison, my father furiously striking the floor with his cane. And my brother with his sack of fruit.

In the depths of my suffering, I was still trying to understand why I hadn't seen anything when the fire reached my head. There had been a gasoline can next to me, but there was a cork in it. I didn't see Hussein pick it up. My head was down when he said he was going to "take care of me" and for a few seconds I thought I was saved because of his smile and the blade of grass he was calmly chewing. In reality, he wanted to gain my confidence to keep me from running away. He had planned everything the day before with my parents. But where did the fire come from? The coals? I didn't see anything. Did he use a match to do it so quickly? I always had a box next to me, but I didn't see that, either. So it must have been a lighter in his pocket. Just enough time to feel the cold liquid on my hair, and I was already in flames. I would so much like to know why I didn't see anything.

It's a nightmare without end at night, lying flat on my back on this bed in the hospital. I am in total darkness, I see curtains around me; the window has disappeared. I feel a strange pain like a knife stuck into my stomach, my legs tremble. I am dying. I try to sit up but can't. My arms are still stiff, two filthy wounds that are of no use. There is no one, I am alone. Then who stuck this knife into my stomach?

I feel something strange between my legs. I bend one leg, then the other, I try to disengage this thing that frightens me. I don't realize, at first, that I'm giving birth. I feel around in the darkness with my two feet. Without really knowing what it is, I push the child's body slowly back under the sheet. I stay still for a moment, exhausted by the effort.

When I bring my legs together, I feel the baby against the skin on both my legs. It moves a little. I hold my breath. How did it get out so quickly? A knife stab in the belly and it's there? I'm going back to sleep, it's impossible, this child didn't come out all alone without warning. I must be having a nightmare.

But I'm not dreaming, because it's there, between my knees, against the skin of my legs. They weren't burned so I have sensation in my legs and my feet. I don't move, then I raise a leg, the way you would with an arm, to brush a tiny head, arms that move feebly. I must have cried out. I don't remember. The doctor comes into the room, parts the curtains, but I'm still in darkness. It must be night outside. I see only a light in the hall through the open door. The doctor leans over and he takes the baby away, without even showing it to me. There's nothing between my legs now. Someone pulls the curtains closed. I don't remember anything more. I must have fainted, I slept a long time, I don't know. The next day and the following days, I am certain of only one thing: The child is no longer in my belly.

I didn't know if he was dead or alive, no one spoke to me about it, and I didn't dare ask the unkind nurse what they had done with this child. May he forgive me, I was incapable of giving him a reality. I knew that I had given birth but I hadn't seen him, he wasn't put into my arms, I didn't know if it was a girl or a boy. I was not a mother at this moment, but human debris condemned to death. My strongest emotion was shame.

The doctor told me later that I had given birth at seven months to a tiny baby, but that he was alive and being cared for. I vaguely heard what he was saying to me, my ears had been burned and hurt so terribly! I was in pain all over the upper part of my body, and I kept passing from a coma to a half-awake state, with no awareness of day or night. They were all hoping for me to die and they expected it to happen. But I found that God would not have me die so quickly. The nights and days were confused in the same nightmare and in my rare moments of lucidity I had only one obsession, to rip with my nails this infected stinking skin. Unfortunately, my arms wouldn't obey me.

Someone came into the room once, in the middle of this nightmare. I sensed a presence rather than actually seeing someone. A hand passed like a shadow over my face without touching it. A woman's voice with a peculiar accent said to me in Arabic: "I'm going to help you, do you understand?" I said yes, without believing it. I was so uncomfortable in that bed, the object of everyone's scorn, I didn't understand how anyone could help me, especially how anyone could have the power to help. Bring me back to my family? They didn't want any part of me. A woman burned for honor is supposed to burn to death. The only way to help me stop suffering was to help me die.

But I say yes to this woman. I don't know who she is.

Jacqueline

My name is Jacqueline. At the time of these events, I was in the Middle East working with a humanitarian organization, Terre des Hommes, which was directed by an extraordinary person whose name was Edmond Kaiser. I would tour the hospitals looking for children who had been abandoned, handicapped children, or children suffering from malnutrition. This work is done in collaboration with the International Red Cross and other organizations involved with Israelis and people from the West Bank. I have a great deal of contact with both populations, because I live and work within their communities.

However, it was only after I had been in the Middle East for seven years that I heard about girls being murdered by their own families because they had had contact with a boy. This could have been nothing more than just talking to a boy. The family suspects a girl on anybody's word, sometimes with no proof at all. It does sometimes happen that a girl really has had an "adventure" with a boy, which is absolutely unthinkable in this culture, given that it is the father who makes all decisions about marriage. But until I heard about Souad, I had never actually been involved in such a case.

To a Western mind, the idea that parents or brothers can murder their own daughter or sister simply because she has fallen in love seems unbelievable, especially in these times. In our society, women are free, they vote, they may have children out of wedlock, they choose their husbands.

But having lived here for seven years, the first time someone spoke to me about it, I knew immediately that it was true, even though I had had no personal involvement in such a case. There must be an atmosphere of trust before anyone will even speak of a subject as taboo as this one, which especially does not concern foreigners. It was a woman who decided to bring it up with me, a Christian friend with whom I am frequently in contact because she works with children. She sees many mothers from villages all over the country. She is a little like the neighborhood *moukhtar*, that is, she invites the women to have a coffee or tea and talks with them about what is going on in their village. It is an important form of communication here. You have conversation every day over coffee or tea. The custom gave her the opportunity to make a mental note of the cases of children in serious difficulty that she would hear about. And one day she heard a group of women say that in one of the villages there was a girl who had behaved very badly and whose parents tried to burn her to death. They thought she was in a hospital somewhere.

This friend has a certain charisma, and she is well respected. She displays an enormous courage, which I was about to witness. Normally she is involved only with children, but the mother is never far from the child. So around the fifteenth of September of that year, my friend said to me: "Listen, Jacqueline, there is a girl in the hospital who is dying. The social service worker confirmed to me that she was burned by someone in her family. Do you think you can do something?"

When I asked her what more she knew about the case, she said only that it was a young girl who was pregnant; the villagers said she was rightly punished, and now she was expected to die in the hospital. When I expressed my horror, she said that's the way things are here. The girl was pregnant and so she has to die. That's all there is to it, it's quite normal. Everyone feels so sorry for the poor parents, but not for the girl. Besides, she would die anyway according to what she had heard.

A story like this sounded an alarm in my head. Children were my first mission. I had never become involved in this type of case, and for good reason, but I said to myself: *Jacqueline, old girl, you have to see for yourself what this is about!*

I left for the hospital. It was not a hospital that I was particularly familiar with. However, I know the country and the customs, and I can get along in the language, because I have spent so much time here. I simply asked to be taken to a girl who had been burned. They led the way without any problem, and I entered a large room where I saw two beds, each occupied by a girl. I immediately sensed that it was an isolation unit, a place where they put the cases they don't want seen. It was a rather dark room, with bars on the windows, two beds, and nothing else. As there were two girls, I told the nurse I was looking for the one who had just had a baby. She pointed to one of the girls and then left the room. She didn't stop in the hallway, she didn't ask me who I was, nothing! Just motioned vaguely toward one of the beds: "It's that one!"

One of the girls has short frizzy hair, it looks almost shaved. The other one has medium-length straight hair. But the faces of both girls are blackened, sooty. Their bodies are covered by a sheet. I know they have been here a while, about two weeks according to what I have been told. It is obvious that they are unable to speak. They both look close to death. The one with the straight hair is in a coma. The other one, the one who had the child, opens her eyes from time to time, but just barely.

No one comes into the room, neither nurse nor doctor. I don't dare speak, much less touch them, and the odor that hangs in the air is foul. I have come to see one girl, and I discover two of them, both hideously burned from all evidence, and both without care. I go out to look for a nurse in another ward, and when I find one, I ask to see the medical director of the hospital.

I am familiar with the hospital setting. The medical director receives me well and seems somewhat sympathetic. I mention that there are two girls who have been burned and tell him that I work with a humanitarian organization that could possibly help them.

"Listen. One of them fell into a fire and the other one, it's the family's business. I advise you not to get involved."

I tell him that my work is giving aid, and especially to people who have no other source of help, and ask if he can tell me a little more about it.

"No, no, no. Be careful. Don't get involved in this kind of business!"

When it's like that, you can't force people too much. I leave it at that but I go back down to the isolation room where the girls are being kept and sit down for a moment. I wait, hoping that the girl who opened her eyes a little is able to communicate. The condition of the other one is more disturbing. When a nurse walks by in the hallway, I ask about what happened to the girl, the one who has hair and doesn't move.

"Oh, she fell into a fire and is in very bad shape. She's going to die."

There is no pity in this diagnosis, simply a statement of fact. But I do not accept this standard explanation about falling into a fire.

The other one stirs a little. I move closer to her and stay there a few minutes without speaking. I watch and try to understand the situation; I listen to the sounds in the corridor, thinking someone else will come in, someone with whom I can speak. But the nurses pass by very quickly and they have absolutely nothing to do with these two girls. From all appearances, there is no organized care for them. Actually, there must be a little something, but it isn't apparent. No one approaches me, no one asks me anything. I am, after all, a foreigner dressed in Western-style clothes, yet I am always well covered, out of respect for their traditions; and this respect is indispensable to getting along and getting things accomplished. I think someone might at least ask me what I'm doing there, but instead they ignore me.

After a little while, I lean over this girl who seems able to hear me. But I don't know where to touch her. The sheet prevents me from seeing where she has been burned. I see that her chin is completely stuck to her chest, it's all of a piece. Her ears are burned and not much is left of them. When I pass a hand in front of her eyes, she doesn't react. I can't see her arms or her hands, and I don't dare lift this sheet. But I have to touch her somewhere to make her aware of my presence. As with a dying person, it is important to make her understand that someone is there, so that she may feel a presence, a human contact. Under the sheet, her knees are bent. I place my hand gently on her knee, and she opens her eyes.

"What is your name?" She doesn't answer.

"Listen to me, I'm going to help you. I will come back and I will help you."

"*Aioua*," which means yes in Arabic, and that's all. She closes her eyes. I don't even know if she's seen me.

That was my first visit with Souad. I left feeling overwhelmed. I was going to do something, that much was apparent to me!

In everything I have done up to now, I have always had the feeling of receiving a call. I hear about someone in distress, I go there knowing that I'm going to do something to answer that call. I don't know what, but I'll find a way. So I go back to see that friend, who is able to give me some new information, if you can call it that, about this girl's case. She tells me that the child she gave birth to has already been taken away by the social services by order of the police. The girl is young, no one is going to help me in the hospital. "Jacqueline, believe me, you are not going to be able to do anything." My response is that we'll see.

The next day when I return to the hospital, she is still only semiconscious, and her neighbor in the next bed is still in a coma. And this fetid odor is unbearable. I'm not aware of the extent of her burns but I do know that no one has disinfected them. The following day, one of the two beds is empty. The girl who was in a coma died during the night. I look at this bed, empty but not cleaned with any great care. It's always painful not to have been able to do something, and I tell myself that now it is time to look after the other one. But she is only semiconscious, and I don't understand anything of what she tries to answer me in her delirium.

And here is where what I call the miracle happens, in the person of a young Palestinian doctor whom I see here for the first time. The hospital director already had told me to let it drop because she was dying. I ask this young doctor for his opinion and why they haven't at least cleaned her face.

"They try to clean her as well as they can but it is very difficult. This sort of case is very complicated because of customs . . . you understand."

"Do you think she can be saved, that something can be done?"

"Since she isn't dead yet, there may be a chance. But tread carefully with this type of situation, be very careful."

In the following days, I find a somewhat cleaner face, with streaks of Mercurochrome here and there. The young doctor must have given instructions to the nurse, who makes an effort but not a great one. Souad tells me later that they had held her by the hair to rinse her off in a bathtub, because no one wanted to touch her. I am careful not to criticize, which would only worsen my relationship with this hospital. I go back to see my young Arab doctor, the only person who seems accessible. I tell him about my work with the humanitarian organization and my interest in trying to help, and ask him again if he thinks she has any hope of surviving.

"My opinion is that, yes, she does, something could be attempted, but I don't think it can be done in our hospital."

"Well, could we take her to another hospital?"

"Theoretically, yes, but she has a family, parents. She is a minor and we can't intervene. The parents know she's here, the mother has already come, and besides they have been forbidden visits ever since. It's a very special case, believe me."

"Listen, Doctor, I would like to do something. I don't know what the legal obstacles are, but if you tell me she has a chance to live, even the smallest chance, I can't let the possibility drop."

The young doctor looks at me, a little amazed by my stubbornness. He certainly must think that I don't grasp the situation . . .

one of these "humanitarians" who understand nothing about the country. He is about thirty years old, and I find him sympathetic. He is tall, thin, dark, and he speaks English well. He doesn't at all resemble his colleagues, most of whom are closed to the inquiries of Westerners.

"If I can help you, I will do it."

Success! On the following days, he speaks willingly with me about the patient's condition. Since he was educated in England and is rather cultured, the interactions are easier than usual. I go a little farther in my investigations into Souad and learn that, in effect, she has received no care. The doctor reminds me that she is a minor, that it is absolutely forbidden to touch her without her parents' permission. "And for them she's as good as dead. That's all they're waiting for."

I ask if I might be allowed to put her into another hospital where she will be cared for and better treated. Does he think they will let me do it? He says that only the parents can give permission for that, and they will not authorize me to do it. I go back to see my friend, who was the source of this adventure, and I share my idea with her of having Souad moved somewhere else and ask if she thinks it is possible.

"You know that if the parents want her to die, you won't be able to do anything! It's a question of honor for them in the village."

I can be rather stubborn in this type of situation. If I am dissatisfied with a negative answer, I want to push on until I find an opening, even a tiny one. In any case, I usually pursue an idea to the limits.

"Do you think I can go to this village?"

"You're risking a lot if you go there. Listen to me. You don't know how relentless this code of honor is. They want her to die,

126

because if she doesn't, their honor has not been washed clean and the family is rejected by the village. They would have to leave in disgrace. Do you understand? You can always throw yourself into the lion's jaws, but in my opinion you are taking a big chance for probably no results in the end. She is condemned. Without any care for such a long time, with burns like these, the poor girl won't live long."

But the next time I go to see this little Souad, she opens her eyes a little, and she listens to me and answers me with a few words despite her dreadful suffering. When I ask her where her baby is, she says she does not know, they took it away. With what she is enduring, and what awaits her, seemingly imminent death, I understand very well that the child is not her major problem.

"Souad, you have to answer me, because I want to do something. If we are able to get you out of here, if I can take you somewhere else, will you come with me?"

"Yes, yes, yes. I'll come with you. Where will we go?"

"To another country, I don't know where, but someplace where all this will be behind you."

"Yes, but my parents . . ."

"We'll see about your parents. We'll see. Agreed? You trust me?"

"Yes . . . thank you."

So, armed with this confidence, I ask the young doctor if he knows where this famous village is where they incinerate young girls who are guilty of being in love.

"She comes from a little hamlet, about forty kilometers from here. It's rather far and there's hardly any passable road. It's also dangerous, because you don't know exactly what goes on there. There aren't any police in these remote places."

"I don't know if I can go there alone . . ."

"Oh no! I don't advise that at all. Even trying to find the place you'll get lost ten times over. There aren't any maps sufficiently detailed . . ."

I may be naive but I am not stupid. I know that it is quite a problem asking for directions on these roads when you're a foreigner. All the more so because the village in question is in territory occupied by the Israelis. And I, Jacqueline, Terres des Hommes or not, humanitarian or not, Christian or not, I could quite easily be taken for an Israeli woman come to spy on the Palestinians, or the opposite, depending on the section of road where I happened to be.

I ask if he will help me by coming along.

"That's madness!"

"Listen, Doctor, we could be saving a life. You tell me yourself that there is some hope if she's taken somewhere else."

To save a life. The argument makes sense to him because he is a doctor. But he is also from this country, like the nurses. And as far as the nurses are concerned, Souad or any other girl like her should die. One has not survived already. I do not know if she even had a chance to pull through but in any case she received no care. I would like to say to this sympathetic doctor that I find it unacceptable to withhold care from a young girl because it is according to custom! But I won't do that, because I know that he himself is caught in this system, vis-à-vis his hospital, his director, the nurses, the population itself. He has already shown great courage in just talking to me about it. Honor crimes are a taboo subject.

But I guess I finally have him half convinced. He is truly a good man; I am touched when he says hesitantly that he doesn't know if he has the courage. I answer that we can only try, and if it doesn't work, we'll just come back.

"All right, but you'll let me turn around if there's the slightest complication?"

I promise him, the young doctor whom I will call Hassan, who is going to be my guide.

I was a young Western woman who had been working in the Middle East to care for children in distress, be they Muslims, Jews, or Christians. This is always a complicated exercise in diplomacy. But the day I got into my car with this brave doctor at my side, I didn't really appreciate the risk I was running. The roads were not safe, the inhabitants were mistrustful, and I was bringing along an Arab doctor, freshly graduated from an English university, on an adventure that would be incredible if the goal were not so serious. He must have found me completely mad.

When we leave in the morning, Hassan is a little green with fear. I would be lying if I said I am at ease, but with the daring of youth at the time, and the conviction of my engagement in the service of others, I plunge ahead. Obviously neither of us is armed.

For me it's "God be with us," for him, it's "Inshallah!"

When we leave the city, we are driving in a classic Palestinian countryside, with parcels of land that belong to small farmers. The parcels are surrounded by low stone walls, with little lizards and snakes running between the stones. The land, which is a reddish ocher color, is dotted with fig trees. The road that leads out from the city is not blacktopped but it is passable. It connects the hamlets, the neighboring villages, and the markets. The Israeli tanks have just about flattened it but there remain enough holes to make my little car rattle. The farther you get from the city, the more you see small farms. If the parcel of land is big enough, the farmers grow wheat, but in the smaller ones they let the flocks graze, a few goats, some sheep, more animals if the farmer is rich. The girls labor in the fields. They attend school very little, if at all, and those who are lucky enough to go are soon brought back to take care of the younger ones. I had quickly understood that Souad is completely illiterate.

Hassan knows this road but we're looking for a village that he has never heard of. From time to time we ask directions but because my car has an Israeli license plate it puts us in some danger. We are in occupied territory and the directions we are given are not necessarily reliable.

After a short time, Hassan says to me: "This is crazy, we're going to be all alone in this village. I forewarned the family by the Arab telephone, but God knows how they'll receive us. The father by himself? The whole family? Or the whole village? They can't possibly understand your involvement!"

"Did you tell them that the girl is going to die and that we're coming to talk to them about it?"

"Exactly, that's just what they're not going to understand. They burned her, and the one who actually did it is probably waiting for us at the next bend. In any case, they're going to say that her dress caught fire, or that she fell into the coals headfirst! It's complicated in these families . . ."

I know that. From the very first, people have been telling me that a woman who has been burned, that's a complicated situation, and that I shouldn't get involved. Except here I am, involved.

"I'm telling you it would be much better to turn back . . ."

I stimulate my precious companion's courage. Without him I probably would have come anyway, but it is better if a woman doesn't go about alone in these regions. Finally, we arrive at the village in question. The father receives us outside, in the shade of an immense tree in front of the house. I sit down on the ground with Hassan on my right. The father is seated against the tree in a familiar posture with one leg bent, on which his cane rests. He's a small man, reddish hair, a very pale face with freckles, somewhat albino looking. The mother remains standing, very erect in her black dress, a veil of the same color on her head. Her face is uncovered. She is an ageless woman, with strong features, a hard expression. Palestinian peasant women often have this look. But with what they endure, their burden of work, children, and servitude, it is understandable.

The house is of medium size, very typical of the region, but we don't see much of it. Seen from the outside, it has a closed look. In any case, the man is not poor.

Hassan introduces me with a local expression of politeness. "This woman works for a humanitarian organization."

And the conversation goes along in the Palestinian style, first between the two men: "How are your flocks doing? And the harvest? You sell well?"

"The weather's bad. Winter's coming. The Israelis make a lot of problems for us."

They talk about the weather for some time before touching on the real subject of our visit. That's customary. He does not mention his daughter, so Hassan does not say anything about her, and neither do I. They offer us tea. Since I'm a stranger, I cannot refuse the customary hospitality. And then it's time to go. Goodbyes.

"We'll come back to pay you another visit."

We are not going to get any farther than that today and so we leave. It is necessary to begin like this, both of us know that. We have to broach the subject very slowly and not appear to be enemies, or inquisitors, give it a little time, in order to be able to return. And there we are again on the road going toward the city. I remember the sigh of relief that escaped me. I felt like I had been walking on eggs.

"That didn't go too badly, did it? We'll go back in a couple of days."

"You really want to go back?"

"Yes, we haven't accomplished anything yet."

"But what do you hope to offer them? If it's money, that's no good, don't count on it. Honor is honor."

"I'm going to play up that she's dying. It's unfortunately true and you said so yourself."

"Without emergency care, and the emergency is already past, she scarcely has any chance."

"Well, since she can't remain there, I am going to tell them that I will take her somewhere else to die. That could be arranged and would relieve them of the problem."

"She's a minor and she hasn't any papers. The parents' agreement is needed. They won't budge for the papers, you won't get what you want."

"We'll go back anyway. You'll ring up on the Arab telephone when?"

"In a few days. Give me some time."

She doesn't have any time, little Souad. But Hassan, besides being a miracle doctor for my expedition, has his job at the hospital, a family, and the simple fact that getting involved in an honor crime can bring him serious enemies. I understand him more and more and I respect his caution. To attack a taboo of this type, or even try to work around it, this is new for me, and I put all my energy into it. But he's the one who has to make contact in the village to announce our visits, and I can well imagine the force of persuasion he has to employ for this simple task.

Souad Is Going to Die

"My brother is nice. He tried to bring me bananas and the doctor told him not to come back."

"Who did this to you?"

"My brother-in-law, Hussein, my older sister's husband. My mother brought poison in a glass . . ."

I know a little more about Souad's story. She is able to speak to me better, but the conditions in this hospital are terrible for her. The burns are becoming infected, they weep and bleed continuously. I notice the upper part of her body: Her head is always lowered as if in prayer, her chin is attached to her chest. She can't move her arms. The gasoline was poured over her head, and it burned her as it ran down her ears and neck, over her back, arms, and upper chest. She rolled up in a ball like a strange mummy, probably when they were transporting her, and she is still in this same position more than two weeks later. That is not even considering the effects of giving birth in a semicoma, and then the child who has disappeared. The social worker must have deposited him like a pathetic little package in some orphanage, but where? And

I know only too well the future that awaits these illegitimate children. He has no hope.

My plan is crazy. I first want to bring her to Bethlehem, a city under Israeli control at this time, but accessible for both of us. I know for a fact that they don't have the means of caring for serious burn patients, but this is only a first step. They can at least dispense the minimal basic care. The next phase of the plan: leave for Europe, with the agreement of Terres des Hommes, which I have not yet requested. And all of this does not yet include the child, whom I intend to try to find in the meantime.

When my young doctor gets into my little car for a second visit to the parents, he is still uneasy. Same welcome, still outside under the tree, same banal conversation as we get up to leave, but this time I mention the children that we never see.

"You have many children? Where are they?"

"They're in the fields. We have a married daughter, she has two boys, and a married son, who also has two boys."

Boys, that's good. You have to congratulate the head of the family. And extend your sympathy, as well: "I know that you have a daughter who is the cause of much trouble for you."

"*Ya haram!* It's terrible what's happened to us! What misery!"

"It's really a pity for you."

"Yes, a pity. *Allah karim!* But God is great."

"In a village, it is painful to have such problems . . ."

"Yes, very hard for us."

The mother does not speak, always standing solemn and motionless.

"Well, fine," I say, "she's going to die soon anyway. She's in very bad shape."

"Yes. *Allah karim!*"

And my doctor adds, very professional: "Yes, she is very bad."

He understands my participation in this strange bargaining over the hoped-for death of a young girl. He helps me by adding explicit comments about Souad's inevitable death, while we are hoping for the opposite. The father finally takes the bait and confides in him the core of all their worries: "I hope we will be able to stay in the village."

"Yes, of course. In any case, she's going to die."

"If Allah wills it. It's our fate. We can't do anything about it."

But he does not say what happened, nothing at all. So I advance a pawn on the chessboard and say, "But all the same, it's a pity for you that she is dying here. How do you plan to bury her? Where?"

"We'll bury her here in the garden."

"Perhaps if I took her with me, she could die elsewhere and you wouldn't have any problems like that."

This clearly means nothing to them, my taking her with me to die somewhere else. They have never in their lives heard of such a thing. Hassan understands this and he pursues it: "She is right. All in all, that would mean fewer problems for you, and for the village."

"Yes, but we will bury her like that, if Allah wants it so, and we will say to everyone that we buried her and that will be that."

"I don't know, just think about it. Perhaps I can take her to die somewhere else. I can do that if it would be good for you."

It is frightful, but I can only keep emphasizing her death in this morbid game. To help Souad live again and speak of medical care would horrify them. They tell us they need to talk about it among themselves. This is their way of signaling that it is time for us to leave, which we do after the customary good-byes, promising to return. What should we think now about our attempt? Have we negotiated properly? We think our offer makes sense. On the one hand, Souad disappears, on the other, the family recovers their honor in the village.

Allah is great as the father says. We must be patient.

During this time, I go to the hospital every day to try to get Souad at least the minimum of care. My presence obliges them to make a little effort. For example, they disinfect the burns somewhat more frequently. But without painkillers and without specialized products for treating severe burns, poor Souad's skin remains an immense wound, unbearable for her and difficult for others to see. I think about the hospitals in Switzerland, and France, and other places where they treat burns with such gentle and exquisite care to help the skin regenerate with a minimum of scarring and make the pain bearable.

And we return to the negotiating, always just the two of us, my courageous doctor and I. We stick with it, we set out the terms with as much diplomacy as possible: "What would not be good would be for her to die in this country. Even there in the hospital that would not be good for you. But she can be taken far away, to another country. And that way, it's over, finished, you can tell the whole village that she has died. She will have died in another country and you'll never again hear a word about her."

The conversation is more than strained at this moment. Without papers, any agreement with them is worth nothing to me. I'm almost there. I ask nothing else about the situation, neither who did this nor who the father of the child is. These details do not enter into the negotiation, and bringing them up would only further sully the family's honor. My interest is in convincing them that their daughter *is* going to die, but somewhere else. And I must seem like a crazy eccentric foreigner, but also someone who in the end might be of use to them.

It seems that the idea is taking root. If they say yes, then as soon as we have turned our backs, they can declare the death of their daughter to the entire village, without any other details, and without the need for a burial in the garden. They will be able to say whatever they want, even that they have avenged their honor in their own way. This is all very bizarre from a Western perspective, to even imagine such discussions. This bargaining does not disturb them morally. Here there is a special kind of morality, enacted against girls and women. The moral sense and legal structures do not protect females; they are based only on the interests of the men of the clan. This mother accepts it herself, without flinching she wishes for the death and disappearance of her own daughter. She cannot do otherwise, and I even find myself feeling sorry for her. Otherwise, I do not get emotionally involved. In all the countries where I work, whether in Africa, India, Jordan, or the West Bank, I have to adapt to the culture and respect ancestral traditions. The unique goal is to bring aid to the woman or man who is the victim. But it is the first time in my life that I have negotiated for a life in this fashion.

They finally give in. The father makes me promise, and the mother, too, that they'll never see her again. *"Never again!"*

I promise this to them but to keep this promise I must take Souad abroad, and to do that I need papers for her.

"I'm going to ask you to do something that may seem a little difficult, but I'll be with you and will help you. We have to go together to the office that issues identity and travel documents. I have to take you by car to Jerusalem, you and your wife, for you to sign the papers."

This new obstacle immediately makes them uneasy. Any contact with the Israeli population, and especially with government officials, is a problem for them.

"But we don't know how to write!"

"That is not a problem, your fingerprint will be enough."

"All right, we will come with you."

Before coming back for the parents, I have to prepare the way with the administration officials. Fortunately, I know people in the Jerusalem visa office. I can explain myself, and the clerks there know what I do for children. Besides, it is a child whom I am rescuing. Souad told me that she was seventeen years old, which makes her still a child. I explain to the Israeli employees that I am going to bring the parents of a gravely ill West Bank girl to them, and that they cannot be kept waiting three hours or they will leave without signing anything. These are illiterate people who need me for the formalities. So I will bring them, with a birth certificate if they have one, and the officials will only have to confirm the age of their daughter on the travel document. And I add, pushing my luck one more time, that this girl is going to be leaving with a child, although I still don't know where the child is or how to find it. But for the moment that is not the issue. First things first: My immediate problem is to get the official approval of the parents and to see that Souad receives some care.

The Israeli employee asks me if I know the name of the child's father. I don't, and I see we may have to write on the form that the child is illegitimate. This designation on an official paper unnerves me: "No, don't write illegitimate! His mother is going to another country and your statement of illegitimacy won't be well received where she's going."

This travel document for Souad and the child is not a passport, only a permit to leave the West Bank for another country. Souad will never return here. She will no longer exist in her country, she will have been eliminated, the little burned girl, a phantom. I ask him to please make out two documents, one for the mother and one for the infant. The clerk asks the whereabouts of the child and I tell him I intend to find out.

Time passes and at the end of an hour the Israeli official gives me the green light. And the next day I am on my way to pick up the parents, alone this time, like a grown-up woman. They get into the car in silence, their faces like masks, and we go to the visa office in Jerusalem. For them, this is enemy territory, where they are usually treated as less than nothing. I wait, seated next to them. My presence assures the Israelis that these people have not brought a bomb with them. They know me very well since I've been working in these regions.

Suddenly the employee who authorizes the papers signals to us to approach: "This girl is nineteen years old according to the birth certificate! You told me seventeen!"

"We're not going to quibble over this. It is hardly important if she's seventeen or nineteen."

"Why didn't you bring her along? She has to sign, too!"

"I didn't bring her because she's in a hospital, dying."

"And the child?"

"Listen, drop it. You'll give me a travel document for their daughter, in front of the parents, and they will sign, and one for the child, too. I'll give you all the details, and then I'll come back for the documents."

If the security of the territory is not at issue, the Israeli authorities are cooperative. When I started my humanitarian work, when it took me into the occupied territories, they at first gave me a hard time.

That changed when they came to understand that I also worked with severely handicapped Israeli children. Many of these children are the products of family intermarriage in certain ultra-religious communities in which cousins marry. The children may be born with Down syndrome or severely handicapped. It is the same in some very religious Arab families. My work at that period was essentially focused on this problem in the two communities. It earned me an attitude of acceptance, notably with the administration.

The office of travel documents is situated outside the walls, in the old city of Jerusalem. Here I am now on foot on the way back to the car with the precious document and with the still-silent parents, in the middle of Israeli soldiers armed to the teeth. I am going to bring the parents back to the village just as I found them there, a little red-haired man with blue eyes in a white head scarf, with his cane, and his wife all in black, her eyes focused on the hem of her dress.

It is at least an hour's trip between Jerusalem and the village. The first time I met them I was very afraid, despite my gung-ho demeanor. Now I no longer fear them, I don't judge them, I think only: *Poor people*. We are all the object of a fate that is all our own.

They follow me coming and going without saying a single word. They are a little afraid that the Israelis will make trouble for them. I had told them that they had nothing to fear, and that everything would turn out all right. Apart from a few essential words, we do not have a real conversation. The rest of the family and the inside of the house remain hidden from me. Observing them, it is hard for me to believe that they wanted to kill their daughter. However, even if the brother-in-law did the act, it was they who had made the decision. The same feelings surfaced in me again later with other parents whom I met in similar circumstances. I could never think of them as murderers. These two do not cry, but I have seen parents cry because they are themselves prisoners of this abominable custom, the honor crime. In front of their house, which encloses their secret and their unhappiness, they get out of the car in silence, and I leave the same way. We will not see each other again.

Now there is much to be done. First, I must get in touch with the head of my agency, Edmond Kaiser, who is the founder of Terre des Hommes. I still have not spoken to him about my crazy plan to take Souad to another country. It seemed advisable to finalize the administrative side of things first. Now the time has come to contact him, and when I do, he tells me he has never heard of this type of story.

I summarize the situation for him: "I have a girl who has been severely burned and who recently gave birth. I intend to bring her to Switzerland, but I don't know yet where the baby is. Are you in agreement with all of this?"

"Evidently, I am."

That is what he was like, Edmond Kaiser. A formidable man, with an intuition for urgency. Once the question was asked, the answer was immediately forthcoming. You could speak to him in this straightforward manner.

I am in a hurry to get Souad out of that hospital where she is receiving inadequate care and suffering miserably, but where she and I have the good fortune of having the enormous support of Doctor Hassan. Without his goodness and his courage, I would not have succeeded. So Edmond Kaiser now knows my plan. Doctor Hassan and I decide to take her out at night, discreetly, on a stretcher, with the agreement of the hospital director that no one will see her. I do not know if they pretended she had died during the night, but it is likely.

I lay her down in the backseat of the car. It is three or four in the morning and we are going off to another hospital. At that time, there were not yet the numerous barricades that were installed at the time of the intifada. The trip goes without a problem and we arrive in the early-morning hours at the hospital, where everything has been prepared. The chief of medicine knows about the situation and I have asked that no questions be put to her about her family, her parents, or her village. The facility, which receives donations from the Order of Malta, is better equipped and very much cleaner.

They settle Souad in a room. I come to see her every day while waiting to receive the visas for Europe, and especially waiting for word about the child. Souad doesn't say anything to me about him. It seems that knowing he is alive somewhere is enough. This apparent indifference is perfectly understandable. Suffering, humiliation, anguish, depression, she is psychologically and physically incapable of accepting herself as a mother. It is important to understand the conditions in which an illegitimate child is received, a child born of a disgraced mother who was burned for the sake of family honor. It is better to separate such a child from the community. If it were possible for this baby to live in good conditions in his own country, we would leave him there. For the child, as for the mother, it would be the least painful solution. Alas, it is impossible. This child will endure the presumed shame of his mother in the depths of some orphanage where he will be scorned. We owe it to him to get him out of there, as we are doing for Souad. And she thinks only about leaving and asks me about it during every visit. I tell her we will leave when we have the visas, and not to worry. She complains about the nurses who tear off her bandages without precaution, she yells every time they come near her, she feels mistreated. The quality of care, although more hygienic, is not ideal. But what else is there to do while we wait for the visas? And this type of document always takes time.

During this wait, I make some moves, using my contacts, to find the little one. The friend who brought Souad's case to my attention gets in touch, a little reluctantly, with a social worker, who reports that she knows where the child is and that it is a boy. But she says that I can't just take him away like that, it's impossible. And besides, she thinks I am wrong to want to be encumbered with the child, because he will be an extra responsibility for me, and afterward for the mother. So I discuss it with Souad: "What is your son's name?"

"His name is Marouan."

"Was it you who gave him this name?"

"Yes, I did. The doctor asked me."

She has some moments of lucidity and others of amnesia, which I sometimes have difficulty following. She has forgotten the terrible circumstances of the child's birth, forgotten that they told her it was a boy, and she had never before mentioned a name to me. Suddenly, in answer to a simple question, the response is direct.

I continue in the same direction: "What do you think about this child? I would think we can't leave without Marouan. I'm going to look for him, because we can't leave him here."

She glances up at me, painfully, because her chin is still attached to her chest.

"You think so?"

"Yes, I do. You are going to get out, but you know in what conditions Marouan is going to be living, it will be a hell for him."

He will always be the son of a *charmuta*. The son of a whore. I don't say so, but she must know it. The tone of this *You think so?* is enough for me. It is a positive response. So I begin looking for the child. First I visit one or two orphanages, trying to find a baby who must be about two months old now, and whose first name is Marouan. But I don't see him, and I am not in the best position to locate this child. The social service worker does not like girls like Souad. She is from a good West Bank family that has not repudiated these traditions. But I'll get nowhere without her. So in response to my insistence, and especially to please my friend, she tells me the center where he has been placed. It is more a rat hole than an orphanage, and getting him out of there will be very complicated. He is a prisoner of the system that placed him there.

I undertake some steps, which finally bring results two weeks later. Along the way, I have met intermediaries of every stripe. There are those who would be in favor of the child being submitted to the same fate as his mother. There are those who favor getting rid of a problem and a mouth to feed—some of these children die without any explanation. And then there are those who have some heart and understand my obstinancy. In the end I have in my arms a two-month-old baby, who has a tiny head that is a little pear-shaped and a little bump on his forehead, a result of his premature birth. He was never cared for in an incubator, even though he was born prematurely. He has the traces of the classic jaundice of newborns. I had been afraid he would have serious problems. His mother had been burned like a torch with her child inside her

146

and he was born in nightmarish conditions. He is scrawny but that isn't serious. He looks at me with round eyes, not crying, calm.

I am used to encountering children suffering from malnutrition; we had about sixty of them at the time in an institution where I worked. I bring him home with me where I have everything I'll need for him. I have already had experience traveling with seriously ill children who needed to have an operation in Europe. I place Marouan for the night in a basket, diapered, dressed, fed. I have the visas. I have everything. Edmond Kaiser will be waiting for us in Lausanne to take us directly to the serious burn section of the university hospital.

Tomorrow is the big departure. Souad will be transported on a stretcher to the plane for Tel Aviv. She goes along like a good little girl but she is suffering horribly. When I ask her if she is all right and not in too much pain, she answers simply: "Yes, I am in pain." Nothing more.

"If I turn you a little, will that be better?"

"Yes, that's better. Thank you."

Always *thank you*. Thank you for the wheelchair at the airport, an object she had never seen in her life. Thank you for the coffee with a straw. Thank you for settling her in somewhere while I get the boarding passes. As I am holding the baby and having trouble balancing him while I go through the formalities, I tell Souad that I'm going to place the little one on her and not to move. She gives me a frightened look. Her burns prevent her from taking him in her arms. She manages to bring them just close enough together, stiffly, on both sides of the baby's body. And she makes a fearful gesture when I entrust the baby to her. It is hard for her.

"Stay just like that. I'll be right back."

I am really forced to enlist her help, I can't push the wheelchair, hold the baby, and go to all the counters where I have to show my passport, the visas, the documents for Souad and the baby, and explain my strange traveling group. And it is a nightmare, because the travelers who walk near her do what everyone does before a baby: "Oh, what a beautiful baby! Ah! He's adorable!" They don't even look at the mother, completely disfigured, her head bent over this child. She has bandages under her hospital gown—it was too difficult to dress her—on top of which is one of my woolen jackets and a blanket over that. She can't raise her head to say thank you to the passersby and to tell me how much this baby, whom they find so adorable, panics her. As I move away from her to take care of the official business, I think how surrealistic this scene is. She is there, burned, the baby in her arms. She has experienced hell and so has he, and people pass by with a smile. "Oh, the beautiful baby!"

When it is time to board, another problem presents itself: how to get her on the plane. I have already taken a wheelchair up the steps of an airplane, but here I am really stymied. The Israelis have a technique, however. They bring a huge crane, and Souad is suspended in a sort of cabin at the end of it. The cabin rises slowly, arrives level with the plane's door, and two men are there to receive her.

I have reserved three seats in front to be able to stretch her out, and the flight attendants have arranged a curtain to shield her from the looks of the other passengers. Marouan is in a cradle provided by the airline company. We are on a direct flight to Lausanne. Souad doesn't complain. I try to help her change position from time to time, but nothing soothes her. The pain medication really has not had much effect. She looks a little haggard, half asleep, but confident. I can't get her to eat but I do give her something to drink through a straw. And I look after the baby, who needs changing. She avoids looking at him.

She suffers from so many complications. She doesn't know what Switzerland means, this country where she is going for treatment. She has never seen an airplane before, or a crane, or so many different people in the hubbub of an international airport. She has seen nothing of the world and is suddenly being barraged by all sorts of new experiences that are perhaps terrifying for her. Her suffering is far from at an end. It will require a long time before her survival results in a bearable life. I do not even know if they will be able to operate on her, if skin grafts are still possible. Then there will be the integration into the Western world, learning a language, followed by all the rest of the acculturation. When you "bring out" a victim, as Edmond Kaiser says, you know that it is a responsibility for life.

Souad's head is next to the window. I say to her, "You see those? They're called clouds." I don't think she is capable, in her condition, of thinking about everything that awaits her. She hopes, without knowing for what exactly. She sleeps. Some of the passengers complain about the odor, despite the curtains drawn around her. From the day of my first visit to Souad, in that dreadful hospital room, two months have gone by. Every centimeter of skin on her chest and her arms is decomposed in a vast purulent wound. The passengers can hold their noses and make faces of disgust to the flight attendants, it's all the same to me. I'm taking a burned woman and her child to their salvation, one day they will know why. They will know, too, that there are others, already dead or dying, in every country where the law of men has institutionalized honor crimes—in the West Bank, in Jordan, Turkey, Iran, Iraq, Yemen, India, Pakistan, and even in Israel, and yes, even in

Europe. They will know that the rare ones who escape must spend the rest of their lives in hiding, because their assassins may still be successful.

Most of the humanitarian organizations do not take up the cases of these women, because they are individual social cases, "cultural" cases! And because in some countries, laws protect the murderer. Their cases do not excite the big campaigns that are waged against famine and war, to aid refuges, or battle epidemics. I can understand and acknowledge this sad situation in the world. The experience I lived demonstrates the difficulty and the time needed to discreetly implant oneself in a country to recover the victims of honor crimes and help them, and the risks and perils involved. Souad is my first rescue of this type, but this endeavor is a long way from finished: Keeping her from dying is one thing, making her live again is another.

Switzerland (Souad)

As the infant lay across the seats on the plane, I could look at his beautiful little face, long and dark, with his white hospital bonnet on his head. I lost the sense of time and had the impression that it had only been three weeks, when actually Marouan was already two months old. Jacqueline told me that we arrived in Geneva on December 20.

I was so afraid when she first settled him on me. My arms couldn't hold him, and I was in such a state of confusion, shame, and suffering all mixed together that I didn't quite realize what was happening. I slept most of the time and don't even remember getting off the plane and into the ambulance that took me to the hospital. It was only the next day that I began to understand where I was. Of this extraordinary day when I was taken out of my country I have retained only the memory of Marouan's face and seeing the clouds from the airplane. I wondered what those funny white things were on the other side of the window. I did know that we were going to Switzerland, but at the time the word meant nothing to me. I confused Swiss and Jewish, because everything outside my village was one big enemy country.

151

I had no idea about foreign countries and their names. I didn't even know much about my own country outside my village. I was taught that there was my territory and then the rest of the world, the enemy, where "they eat pork!" as my father used to say. That was how evil he thought they were.

But now I was going to live in an enemy country, and with great confidence, because "the lady" was there with me. The people around me in this hospital did not know my story. Jacqueline and Edmond Kaiser had said nothing about it. I was a burn victim, and that was the only thing that mattered in this place. They took charge of me the next day for an emergency operation, which consisted of unsticking my chin from my chest to allow me to raise my head. The flesh was raw; I had lost a lot of weight and now was only thirty kilos of burns and bones, and not much skin. Every time I saw the nurse coming with her instrument table, I would start crying because the procedures, which I knew were necessary, were excruciating. They did give me tranquilizers, and the nurse was very, very gentle. She cut away the dead skin delicately, getting hold of it with a tweezers. She gave me antibiotics, they soothed my burns with creams. There were no horrors of forced showers, gauze ripped off carelessly as I had endured in the hospital in my country. At first, my arms just hung down on either side, stiff like a doll's arms, but eventually they were able to straighten them so that I could move them. I began to stand and then to walk in the halls and to use my hands.

At the same time, I was learning about this new world whose language I didn't speak. Since I didn't know how to read or write even in Arabic, I took refuge in a prudent silence until I got to know some basic words.

I could only express myself with Jacqueline and Hoda, both

women who spoke Arabic. Edmond Kaiser was marvelous. I admired him as I had never in my previous life admired any man. He acted like a *real* father, I now understand, one who had made a decision about my life and allowed Jacqueline to bring me here.

What surprised me very much when I came out of my room to go see Marouan in the nursery was the freedom of the girls. Two nurses went with me, and they were wearing makeup, their hair was nicely styled, they wore short dresses, and they spoke with men. I thought to myself: *They're speaking with men, they're going to die!* I was so shocked that I said so to Jacqueline and Edmond Kaiser as soon as I had the right words.

"Look at that girl over there, she's having a conversation with a man! They're going to kill her."

I made a gesture of slicing my hand across my neck.

"No, they're in Switzerland, it's not the same as in your country. Nobody will harm them. This is normal behavior in the Western world."

"But look, their legs are showing, it's not right to see a girl's legs."

"But yes, it's quite normal."

"And the eyes. It's not a bad thing for women to wear makeup?"

"No, the women here use makeup, they go out, they have the right to have a male friend—very different from your village. You're here, you're not in your land, you're in Switzerland."

This was not easy for me to grasp and get used to. I must have worn out Edmond Kaiser asking him the same questions over and over. The first time, I commented: "That girl, I won't see her again, because she's going to die." But the next day, I saw that she was still there and I was happy for her. I said to myself: *Thank God she is alive. She is wearing the same white blouse, her legs are show-*

ing, so that must be all right, and you aren't punished for that. I had thought that everywhere it was the same as in my village. I was also shocked by the way these girls walked. They were smiling and at ease, and walked with confidence, like men.

And I saw many blonde girls: "Why are they blonde? Why aren't they dark like me? Because there is less sun? When it's warmer they'll become dark and their hair will be curly? Oh! She put on short sleeves. Look over there, those two women who are laughing! Where I come from a woman never laughs with another woman and no woman would ever wear short sleeves. And they have shoes!" I was startled by all of this.

I remember the first time I was able to go to the city, alone with Edmond Kaiser. Jacqueline had already left on a mission. I saw women sitting in restaurants, smoking cigarettes, with their arms uncovered showing beautiful white skin. There seemed to be only blondes with white skin. They fascinated me and I wondered where they came from. In my country, blondes are so rare that the men covet them very much, so I thought these girls might be in danger. Edmond Kaiser gave me my first geography lesson, including the differences in people.

"These women were born blonde, but others are born another color in other countries. But here, in Europe, there are also brunettes, red-haired women with spots on their faces . . ."

"Spots like I have?"

"No, not spots from burns like you. Little brown spots caused by the sun on their white skin."

I watched and I kept looking for a woman like me, and I would say to Edmond Kaiser: "May God forgive me, but I would really like to meet another woman who has been burned. I have never seen one. Why am I the only woman who has been burned?"

Even today I still have this feeling of being the only burned woman in the world. If I had been the victim of an automobile accident, it wouldn't be the same thing. I guess it's fate, and you cannot hold a grudge against fate. All my life I will feel burned and different. I will always have to conceal my scars under long sleeves. I dream of being able to wear open-necked blouses and short sleeves like other women, but I have to wear clothes that button up to the neck. Other women have that freedom. Even if I am able to walk about freely, I am a prisoner in my skin.

One day I asked if I could have a shiny gold tooth, something I had really wanted. Edmond Kaiser answered me with a smile that I should first get better and then we could talk about my teeth. In my village, a gold tooth was something very special. All that shines is marvelous. I must have surprised him with this strange request, because I had nothing of my own and spent most of my time in bed. They took me for walks from time to time between treatments but it was weeks before I was able to take a shower. There was no question of getting dressed before the scars healed. I wore a large loose shirt that covered my bandages. I couldn't read because I didn't know how. I couldn't speak because the nurses didn't understand me, although Jacqueline had left them cards with words written in French and phonetically in Arabic for "eat," "sleep," "bathroom," "bad," "not bad," everything that could be useful to them in taking care of me. When I was able to get up, I would often sit by the window. I watched the city, the lights, and the mountain above. It was magnificent. I contemplated this spectacle with awe. I wanted to be able to go out and walk. I had never seen anything like this and it was all so beautiful.

Every morning, I went to see Marouan. I had to leave my building to get to the nursery. I was cold since I was wearing only the hospital gown, which closed in the back, a hospital robe, and hospital slippers. These and the hospital toothbrush were my only possessions. So I would walk very quickly, as at home, with my head down. The nurse told me to take it more slowly but I didn't want to. I wanted to put on a proud look outside just because I was alive, even though I was still afraid. That was something the doctors and the nurses couldn't do anything about. I felt like the only burned woman in the world. I felt humiliation and guilt and I couldn't get rid of these feelings.

At night, in the hospital, I often had nightmares, and the face of my brother-in-law would come back to me. I felt him move around me, I could still hear him lying to me, saying: *I'm going to take care of you.* And then I would be running in flames. I thought about this during the day, too, and suddenly I would feel an urge to die, to make the suffering stop. Sometimes, lying in my bed, I would think that I should have died because I deserved to. When Jacqueline transported me from the hospital to the airplane for Switzerland, I had the feeling that I was a bag of garbage that she should have thrown into a corner to be left to rot. This notion, the shame of being what I was, recurred regularly.

Very gradually I began to forget about my first life. I wanted to be someone else in this country, to be like these free women I saw all around me and to fit in here as fast as possible. To achieve this, for many years I buried memories. My village, my family were not supposed to exist in my mind. But there was always Marouan, and the nurses who taught me how to give him the bottle, to change him, to be a mother to him for a few minutes each day to the extent I was physically capable. And I hope my son can forgive me, but I had difficulty doing what was asked of me, because unconsciously I felt guilty being his mother. Who could understand this?

I was incapable of really embracing him as my son, of imagining his future with me and the scars from my burns. How would I tell him, later, that his father was a coward? What could I do so he wouldn't feel guilty himself for what I had become, a mutilated body, frightful to look at? Actually, I couldn't picture myself "before." Had I been pretty? Was my skin soft, my arms supple, and my breasts seductive? There were mirrors in the eyes of others and I saw myself as ugly and to be scorned. A bag of garbage. I was still in a state of acute suffering. While my body was being cared for and I was regaining my physical strength, in my mind things were not always well. Not only did I not know how to express this, but the word *depression* was completely unknown to me. I became acquainted with it some years later. At the time, I just thought that I should not feel sorry for myself and in this way I buried twenty years of my life so deeply that I still have trouble bringing up memories. I think this was necessary in order for me to survive.

For long months there were skin grafts, twenty-four operations in all. My legs, which hadn't been burned, served for replacement skin. Between grafts, it was necessary to wait for the skin to heal and then begin again. Until I had no more skin left to give. The grafted skin was still fragile, I had to take great care to soften and hydrate it. I still have to do that today.

Edmond Kaiser had decided that I should start wearing real clothes. He took me to a department store that was so large and so big and so full of shoes and clothes that I did not know where to look. For shoes, I didn't want embroidered slippers like we wear at home. And I wanted real pants, not a *saroual*. I had already seen girls wearing them when I went in the van with my father when we brought the fruits and vegetables to market. Some girls wore pants that were in style, very wide at the bottom, called

"Charleston" pants. They were considered to be bad girls, and I couldn't wear such things.

I didn't get my "Charlestons." He bought me a pair of black shoes with little heels, jeans, and a very pretty pullover. I was disappointed. I had been dreaming about these new clothes for nine months. But I smiled and I said thank you. I had gotten into the habit of smiling at people all the time, which surprised them, and saying thank you for everything. Smiling was my response to their kindness, but also my only means of communicating for a long time. If I cried, I hid it, an old habit. To smile was the sign of another life. Here people were smiling, even the men. I wanted to smile as much as possible. And having people say thank you to me was a new experience. No one had ever said it to me before, not my father, my brother, or anyone, when I worked like a slave. I was used to being struck, not thanked.

I realized that saying thank you was an act of great politeness and respect and it gave me pleasure to say it because others also said it to me. Thank you for the bandages, for the sleeping pill, for the cream to keep me from tearing off my skin, for the meal, and especially for the chocolate. It's so good, so comforting. I said thank you to Edmond Kaiser for the pants, the shoes, and the pretty pullover. "You're a free woman here, Souad, you can do what you want to do, but I advise you to dress simply, in clothes that suit you and don't irritate your skin, and that don't bring attention to yourself."

He was right. In this country that welcomed me with so much goodness, I was still a little shepherd from the West Bank, without any training or education and without family. And who was still dreaming of a gold tooth!

At the end of the first year after my arrival, I left the hospital to be placed in a shelter. There were more skin grafts, for which I returned to the hospital. It didn't always go well in my mind, but I survived and I couldn't ask for anything better. I was learning French as well as I could, expressions, bits of sentences that I repeated like a parrot, without even knowing what they meant.

Jacqueline explained to me later that when she brought me to Europe, it was more important to save my skin than to send me to school. My repeated hospitalizations did not allow me to take regular French courses. I hadn't even thought about that since in my village there were only two girls who took the bus to go to school in the city, and people made fun of them. Me, too, I ridiculed them, convinced as my sisters were that they would never find a husband if they went to school! Secretly, my greatest shame was not having a husband. I retained the mentality of my village, it was ingrained in me. And I told myself that no man would want anything to do with me. For a woman in my country, living without a man is a punishment for life.

In the shelter that had welcomed me and Marouan, everyone thought I was going to get used to this double punishment of being repulsive to look at and no longer being desired by a man. They also thought I was going to be able to take care of my son and raise him once I was able to work. Only Jacqueline realized that I was totally incapable of doing this, first because it would take me years to become a human being again and to accept myself as I was, and during these years the child was going to grow up the wrong way. Also, despite my twenty years, I was still basically a child myself. I knew nothing about life and responsibilities and certainly nothing about independence.

It was at that time that we left Switzerland. My treatments had been completed so I could now go live elsewhere. Jacqueline found me a foster family somewhere in Europe. This couple became my adoptive parents. I really loved them and called them Papa and Mama, as did Marouan and all the other children. The family took in many children who came from all over the world, and I remember that at one time there were eighteen of us around the table. They were for the most part abandoned children. These amazing people received from Terre des Hommes the money necessary for the temporary shelter of some of the children, and when the children left, it was always painful. I saw some of them throw themselves into the arms of Papa and Mama, they didn't want to leave. For many of them this house was only a temporary home, intended to give them a chance to be healed or cured. Some stayed with our parents for the time needed for an emergency operation, which it would not have been possible to have in their own country, and then they would return home.

The older ones were expected to take care of the smaller ones, and I helped out as best I could. But one day, Mama told me that I was paying too much attention to Marouan and not enough to the others. This surprised me because I didn't have the feeling that I was devoting myself to my son. I felt too lost for that. In my few moments of solitude, I would walk along the river pushing Marouan in his pram. I needed to walk, to be outside. I don't know why I had such a need to walk alone in the country, perhaps the habit of leading the flock at home when I would bring along a little water and something to eat. I did that now as I pushed the pram, walking fast, upright and proud. I walked fast as I had at home, and upright and proud as in Europe.

I did everything possible to do what Mama said, to spend more time caring for the other children. I was the oldest, so it was expected. But as soon as I was closed up in the house, I would be dying to run away, to get out to see other people, to speak, to dance, to meet a man, to see if I could still be a woman. I needed this proof. I was crazy to hope for it, but it was stronger than me. I wanted to try to live.

Marouan

Marouan was five years old when I signed the papers that allowed our foster parents to adopt him. I had made some progress in their language—I still didn't know how to read or write, but otherwise I was able to function. It was not abandonment. My foster parents were going to raise this little boy in the best way possible. And in becoming their son, he was going to benefit from a real education, and bear a name that would protect him from my past. I was completely incapable of caring for him, of providing him equilibrium or even normal schooling. I feel guilty, many years later, for making this choice. But these years have permitted me to construct a life that, back when Marouan was five, I no longer believed in but all the while had hoped for as if by some instinct. I don't know how to explain these things very well, at least not without breaking down in tears. For all these years, I have wanted to convince myself that I wasn't suffering from this separation. But you can't forget your child, especially this particular child.

I knew that he was happy, and he knew that I existed. At the age of five, how could he not know that he had a mother? We had lived together in his adoptive parents' house. But I didn't know how they had explained my departure.

Many of the children in my foster family had a real family and a real country of their own somewhere in the world. Those who had nowhere else to go, like Marouan and me, were adopted. I was legally dead in the West Bank, and Marouan didn't exist there. He was born here, just as I was, on the twentieth of December, the day we arrived in Switzerland. And his parents were also mine. It was a rather strange situation, and when I left this family home, at the end of almost four years of communal life, I thought of myself almost like Marouan's big sister. I was twenty-four years old. I couldn't stay in their charge any longer. I had to work and gain my independence, and finally become an adult.

If I hadn't decided to leave him there and to have him adopted, I would not have been able to raise him alone. I was a depressed mother, I would have brought my suffering on him, my hatred of my family. I would have had to tell him about things I wanted so much to forget! This way Marouan would be sheltered from my personal war.

I couldn't do it, couldn't keep Marouan, it was beyond my strength. I was a refugee, I had no money, I was sick. I would have to live under a false identity the rest of my life because I came from a village where men are cowardly and cruel. And I had every-thing to learn. The only way I could survive was to throw myself into this new country and its customs. I said to myself: *I am here now, I must integrate myself into this country, I haven't any choice.* I didn't want the country to take me in, it was for me to fit in, for me to remake myself. My son spoke the language, he had Euro-pean parents, papers, a normal future, all the things I'd never had and that still were not mine.

I chose to survive and to let him live. I knew from my own experience that this family would be good for him. When they talked to me about adoption, they suggested other families might take him, but I refused: "No, not another family! Marouan will stay here or nothing. I lived with you, I know how he'll be raised here, I don't want him to be placed in another family." Papa gave me his word. I was twenty-four years old, but my mental age probably was not quite fifteen. Too much suffering kept me stuck in childhood. My son was part of a life that I had to forget in order to build another one. At the time, I couldn't understand things this clearly. I went from day to day as in a fog, feeling my way along. But I was certain of one thing, that my son had a right to normal parents and to a safe life, and I was not a normal mother. I hated myself, I wept over my burns, this horrible skin, which condemned me for life. At the beginning, in the hospital, I believed that all these wonderful people were going to give me back my skin. When I realized that I would be in this nightmarish skin for the rest of my days, I retreated deep inside myself. I was nothing anymore, I was ugly, I had to conceal myself so as not to upset people by my appearance. In the years that followed, getting back a taste for life little by little, I wanted to forget Marouan. I was certain he was more fortunate than I was. He was going to school, he had parents, brothers, a sister, and he should be happy. But he was always there, hidden away in a corner of my mind.

I would close my eyes, and there he was. I would see myself running in the street and he was there, behind me, in front or next to me, as if I was running away and he was chasing me. I always had this image of the child whom a nurse placed on my knees, the child I couldn't take in my arms, because of the garden where I ran in flames, and my child burning with me. A child whose father didn't want him, who knew very well that he was condemning both of us to death. And I had loved this man and hoped for so much from him! I was afraid of not finding another man, because of my scars, my face, my body, and what I was inside myself. Always this idea that I was worth nothing, this fear of displeasing, of seeing people look away.

I began by working on a farm, and then thanks to Papa I was hired by a factory that made precision pieces. The work was clean, and I was paid well. I checked printed circuits, parts of mechanisms. There was another interesting area of the factory but you had to check the pieces on a computer and I didn't feel able to do that. I turned down training for this position, pretending that I preferred to work standing on the line, rather than sitting down. One day the head of the team called me: "Souad? Come with me, please."

"Yes, ma'am."

"Sit down, next to me, hold this mouse, I'm going to show you how to do it."

"But I've never done this, I'm not going to know how. I prefer the line . . ."

"And if one day there's no more work on the lines? Then what? Nothing at all? No more work for Souad?"

I didn't dare refuse. Even if I was afraid. Every time I had to learn something new, my hands would get damp and my legs would tremble. I was in a total panic but I gritted my teeth. Every day, every hour of my life, I had to learn new things. I couldn't read or write like the others, and I knew next to nothing of the world. But I wanted so much to work that this woman could have told me to put my head in a bucket and stop breathing and I would have done it. So I learned how to use a mouse and to make out a computer screen. And after a few days, it was all right, and they were all very pleased with me.

I never missed a minute of work in three years, my station was always impeccable, I cleaned it before I left every day, and I was always on time, always there before the others. They had trained me in my childhood, with a stick, to intensive work and to obedience, to exactitude and cleanliness. It was second nature, the only thing that stayed with me of my former life. I would say to myself that you never know, suppose someone were to come by unexpectedly, I wouldn't want them to find the place dirty. I even became a little obsessive about order and cleanliness. An object should be taken from its place and put back, you take a shower every day and change your underwear, you wash your hair twice a week, keep your nails clean. I look for purity everywhere, it's very important to me, and I can't explain it.

I especially like selecting my clothes, but I know this is because choice had always been forbidden me. I like the color red, for example, because my mother would say: "Here's your dress. Put it on." It was ugly and gray but even if I didn't like it, I put it on. So I love red, green, blue, yellow, black, maroon, all the colors I could never have. I don't have much choice about the style of my clothes. Rolled collar, or high neckline, tailored shirt buttoned up, pants. And the hair over the ears. I can't show anything. Sometimes, I would go sit on the terrace of a café, bundled up in my clothes, winter and summer, and I would watch the people pass by. The women in miniskirts or low necklines, arms and legs exposed to the gaze of men. I watched for a man who might look at me but I never found one, so I would go home.

Until the day when I saw from the window of my room a car, and a man inside I couldn't see except for the hands and knees. I fell in love. He was the only man in the world. I saw only him, because of this car, and his two hands on the steering wheel. I didn't fall in love with him because he was handsome, nice, tender, because he didn't hit me or because I was safe with him. I fell in love because he drove a car. Just seeing his car parking in front of the apartment building made my heart beat fast. To be there, simply to see him get into and out of this car when he would leave for work, or return . . . I wept over him! I was afraid in the morning that he wouldn't come back at night.

I didn't realize that it was the same thing as the first time. It took someone to draw it to my attention later for me to realize it. A car and a man who leaves and comes back in it under my window, a man I was in love with before I had even spoken to him, a man I spied on with the anguish of fearing the car might not come back. It was simple. At the time, I hadn't examined these feelings. Sometimes I tried to work through my memories, to know the why of things in my life, but I dropped it very quickly, it was too complicated for me.

Antonio had a red car. I stayed at my window until it disappeared from view, and I would close the window. I met him, I spoke to him. I knew he had a girlfriend, someone I also knew. And then I waited. At first, we became friends. Two and a half or three years went by before the friendship turned into something else. I was in love, but I wasn't sure what he thought of me and I didn't dare ask him. I did everything possible to make him love me, to keep him. I wanted to give him everything, to serve him, to spoil him, feed him, do everything to make him keep me! I couldn't see any other way. How could I seduce him? With my beautiful eyes? My shapely legs? My lovely bosom? How?

We first lived together, without getting married, and it took me some time to be comfortable with him. For example, I couldn't have a light on when I was getting undressed, just candles. In the morning, I closed myself up in the bathroom as fast as possible, and I would only appear covered in a robe from head to foot. And that went on for a long time. Even now it bothers me to be undressed in the light because I know my scars are unattractive.

Our first apartment was a studio in the city. We both worked and made a good living. I waited for him to ask me to marry him but he didn't talk about it. I dreamed about a ring and a ceremony, and all the while I did for Antonio what my mother did for my father, what all the women of my village did for their husbands. I would get up at five o'clock in the morning just for him, to wash his feet and hair and to lay out his clean and well-pressed clothes. Then I watched him leave for work with a departing wave of his hand, a kiss through the window. In the evening, I would wait for him with the meal ready, sometimes until twelve thirty at night or one o'clock in the morning, just to be able to eat with him. Even when I was very hungry, I waited for him as I had seen women do at home. The difference was that I had chosen this man and I loved him. No one had forced him on me. I'm sure it was rather surprising to him, a Western man, who was not used to this type of devotion. In the beginning he would say to me: "This is super! Thank you, it gives me extra time, and I don't have to worry about anything." He was happy. When he came home in the evening, he would sit in his armchair and I would remove his shoes and his socks and give him his slippers. I put myself entirely at his service to keep him at home. I was so afraid every day that he would meet another woman. Then when he did return in the evening and eat the meal I had prepared for him, I was relieved and happy until the next day.

But Antonio didn't want to get married and he didn't want children. I was the one who wanted both of these things. He wasn't ready and I respected that. We lived almost seven years this way. Antonio knew that I had had a child, and that he had been adopted. I had to tell him the essential details of my life to explain my scars, but once I told him, we never spoke about it again. Antonio thought I had chosen the best solution for the child. My son, Marouan, belonged to another family, and I had nothing to say about his life. Although they sent me news about him fairly regularly, I was afraid to go to see him. In fact, I went only three times during all these years, and as quietly as possible. I finally got used to the added burden of guilt. I forced myself so diligently to forget and I almost succeeded. However, I did want a child. But first we would have to marry, that was a must. I had to remake my life in this order: a husband, and then a family.

I was almost thirty years old the day of this much-anticipated marriage. Antonio was ready to go ahead with it because his situation had improved and we could move from a studio into a larger apartment. And he wanted a child, too. It was my first marriage, my first dress, my first beautiful shoes. A long leather skirt and leather blouse, a leather jacket, and high-heeled shoes! Everything was white leather! Leather is so supple, and it is expensive. I loved the sensation of it on my skin. When I would walk through stores, I could never pass a leather garment without touching it, patting it, judging its softness. I had never understood why, but now I know. It is as though I were changing my skin for something soft and smooth. It is a sort of defense, a way of presenting a lovely skin, not my own. Like the smile I usually forced myself to wear as a way of trying to appear pleasant to others.

This marriage was the joy of my life. The only thing close to joy I had known until then was my first rendezvous with Marouan's father. But I no longer thought about that. It was now forgotten, buried in a mind not my own. Then, when I became pregnant, I was in paradise.

Laetitia was a child who was truly wanted. I spoke to her every day she was in my womb. To show off my pregnancy, I wore tight, formfitting clothes. I wanted the world to see my ring to show that I was married and to see that I was expecting a child. This was the complete opposite of what I had experienced the first time, but I didn't realize it then. When I was pregnant with Marouan, I'd had to hide myself, to lie, and to plead to be married so that a child would not be born from my belly and dishonor my family. And now I was alive and free to walk in public with this new child, and I thought I had erased the past with this new happiness. I believed it because I wanted it with all my strength.

Marouan remained hidden in a very small corner of my mind. One day, perhaps, I'd be capable of facing him and telling him everything. But not yet, because I hadn't finished being reborn.

Laetitia arrived like a flower. There was just time to tell the doctor that I thought I needed to go to the bathroom when he said I couldn't because the baby was coming. A little flower with black hair and a smooth complexion, she slipped out of me with remarkable ease. Everyone around me said this was exceptional for a first child, that it is rare to give birth so easily. Of course, it was not my first child! I nursed Laetitia until she was seven and a half months, and she was a very easy baby. She ate everything, she slept well, never a health problem.

Two years later, I wanted another child. Boy or girl, it didn't matter. I wanted it so badly that it didn't happen. The doctor advised Antonio and me to take a vacation and to stop thinking about it and trying so hard. But I was watchful, and I would cry at each disappointment. Finally, I conceived another little girl and we were both wild with joy at the birth of Nadia.

She was still quite small when Laetitia, stroking my hand, asked me, "What is that, Mama, a booboo?"

"Yes, Mama has a booboo, but I'll explain it when you're older."

She didn't mention it again and little by little I would raise my sleeves to let more of myself show. I did this gradually, not wanting her to be shocked or disgusted. She must have been five years old when she touched my arm and asked, "What is that, Mama?"

"Mama was burned."

"What burned you?"

"It was someone."

"He was very bad!"

"Yes, he was very bad."

"Can Papa do to him what he did to you?"

"No, your papa can't do what that person did to Mama, because it was far away, in the country where I was born, and it happened a long time ago. I'll explain all that when you are older."

"But what did he burn you with?"

"You know, in that country, they didn't have washing machines like we have, so Mama would make a fire to do the laundry."

"How did you make the fire?"

"You remember when we went with Papa to get wood in the forest and we made a fire to grill the sausages? Mama did the same thing. I had a place for making a fire to heat the water. And while Mama was doing the washing, a man came and he took a very dangerous liquid, which burns everything, it can even burn down a whole house, and he emptied it on Mama's hair and he lit a match and it caught fire. That's how Mama was burned."

"He's a bad man! I hate him! I'm going to kill him!"

"But you can't go kill him, Laetitia. Perhaps God has already punished him for what he did to me. But that was a long time ago and I'm happy now because I'm with your papa and with you. And you know I love you."

"Mama, why did he do that?"

"It's a very long story and difficult to explain and you're too young to be able to understand."

"But I want to know!"

"No, Laetitia. Mama has told you she will explain it to you someday later. What Mama has just said is enough for now."

That same day, after the evening meal, I was in an armchair and she was standing near me. She stroked my hair and began to raise my sweater. I suspected what she wanted and it made me very uneasy.

"What are you doing, Laetitia?"

"I want to see your back, Mama."

I let her look.

"Ah, Mama, your skin isn't soft like mine."

"Yes, your skin is very soft because it's your real skin, but Mama's skin isn't like that because there is a large scar. That's why you have to be so careful with matches. They're only for lighting Papa's cigarettes. If you touch them you can get burned like Mama. You must promise me that you will be very careful. Fire can kill."

"Are you afraid of fire, Mama?"

I couldn't hide that fear. It would well up in me at the least provocation. And matches were the worst. It's always been that way.

After this, Laetitia began having nightmares and I would hear her thrashing in her bed and crying for help and I saw her clutching her coverlet with all her strength. Once, she even fell out of bed. I hoped that things would calm down, but one day she told me that at night she sometimes would come to my bed to make sure I was just sleeping and not dead. I took her to my doctor because I was worried about her and was upset with myself for telling her too much. But the doctor told me that I had been right to tell her the truth, but that I should pay close attention to her from now on.

And then it was Nadia's turn, more or less at the same age. But she reacted very differently. She did not have nightmares and she wasn't afraid for me. But I could tell that all was not well. It was clear that she kept everything to herself. For instance, we would be sitting together and she would sigh. When I'd ask why she was sighing, she would respond, "I don't know, I just am."

"The heart that sighs does not have what it wants. What do you want to say to Mama that you feel you can't say?"

She surprised me when she said, "Your ears are so little! Do you have little ears because you didn't eat enough?"

"No, honey. Mama has little ears because she was burned."

I explained to Nadia the same way because I wanted both of my girls to hear the same thing, the same words. So I used the same language, the same truth with Nadia. It affected her deeply. Nadia didn't say like her sister that she wanted to kill the person who had done this; she asked to touch my ears. I was wearing earrings, which I often do to hide what remains of my ears.

"You can touch them but please don't pull on the earring because that hurts."

She touched my ears very gently and then she went into her room and closed the door.

I think that the most difficult thing for the girls had to be school. They were getting bigger and Antonio couldn't always go to pick them up so I did this. I imagined the other children's questions: *Why is your mama like that? What's the matter with her? Why does she always wear a sweater in summer? Why doesn't she have any ears?*

The next phase of explanations was harder. I simplified it, without mentioning Marouan. I told them that I had met a man, and we loved each other, but my parents would not allow it. They had decided that I had to be burned and die because this was the custom of my country when a girl disobeyed her parents. But the special lady, Jacqueline, who was known to both Nadia and Laetitia, had brought me to Europe to be healed.

Laetitia was always the more vengeful one, while Nadia was quiet. It was when Laetitia was about twelve that she told me she wanted to go to my village and kill them all. Almost the same words as her father used when I told him my story and about Marouan's birth. "I hope they all die for what they did to you."

My own nightmares returned suddenly. I'd be in bed asleep and Mama would come with a shining knife in her hand. She brandishes it over my head as she says: "I'm going to kill you with this knife!" And the knife shines like a light and my mother is very real, she is standing over me. I would wake up in terror, perspiring, just at the moment when the knife shone the brightest. The most unbearable part was to see my mother. More than death, more than the fire, her face haunts me. She wants to kill me, just as she had killed several of her babies. She is capable of anything, and this is my mother, the woman who gave birth to me!

I was so afraid of resembling her that I decided to have one more operation, but with an aesthetic purpose this time. This one was going to deliver me from a physical resemblance to my mother I could no longer bear to see when I looked in the mirror—a little bump between the eyebrows at the top of the nose—the same as hers. I don't have it anymore, and I think I am more attractive now. But after the surgery, the nightmare continued to haunt me; the surgeon couldn't do anything about that. I should have consulted a psychiatrist, but that idea didn't occur to me then.

One day I went to see a faith healer and explained my case to her. She gave me a tiny knife and told me to put it under my pillow, with the blade closed, and I wouldn't have any more nightmares. I did what she said and the nightmare about the shiny knife did not come back to terrorize me while I slept. Unfortunately, I keep thinking about my mother.

All That Is Missing

I wish so much that I had learned how to write. I can read but only if the letters are printed. I can't read a handwritten letter because I learned by reading the newspaper. When I get stuck on a word, which is often, I ask my daughters.

Edmond Kaiser and Jacqueline had tried to give me some tips in the beginning. I always wanted to learn how to be like the others. Around the age of twenty-four, when I first started to work, I had the opportunity to take a course for three months, which made me very happy. It was difficult because I was paying much more for the course than I was earning. Antonio offered to help me but I wanted to do this with my own money. I stopped after three months but it had really helped me. They taught me to hold a pencil, just as you would teach a child in nursery school, and to write my name. I didn't know how to make an *a* or an *s* so I had to learn the alphabet, letter by letter, at the same time as I was learning to speak the language.

At the end of these three months, I could make out a few words in the newspaper.

I began by reading the horoscopes because someone had told

me that I was Gemini, and every day I would slowly make out my future. What I got out of it wasn't always understandable. I needed briefer texts and short sentences in the beginning. Reading an entire article would have to wait for later. One example of short texts was the death notices. Nobody pored over them as carefully as I did! "The X family regrets to inform of the death of Madame X. May she rest in peace." I also read the short marriage announcements and ads for car sales but I soon gave up on those because abbreviated words were too hard for me. I wanted to subscribe to a popular daily paper but Antonio thought it silly. So every day, before I went to work, I would go into town and start the day by having a coffee and reading the paper. I loved that time of my day. For me it was the best way to learn. And little by little, when people around me talked about some event, I could show that I knew about it, too, because I had read about it in the paper. Now I was beginning to be able to take part in the conversations.

I now know a little of European geography, the big capitals and some smaller cities. In Italy I've seen Rome, Venice, and Portofino and I visited Barcelona, Spain, with my adoptive parents during a summer vacation, but I stayed only five days. I remember it as very hot and I felt I was depriving Papa and Mama of the beach, obliging them to stay inside with me, so I went back and they stayed on. It is hard for me to imagine myself wearing a bathing suit in public. I would have to be alone on the beach as I am when I am undressed in my bathroom.

I have seen a little of the world. I know that it is a round ball but I've never been taught to understand it. For example, I know that the United States is America, but I don't know where this America is on the round ball. I don't even know how to situate the West Bank, my former land, on a map. When I look in my daughters' geography books, I don't know where to begin to grasp the location of all the countries. Part of the problem is that I don't have an understanding of distances. If someone tells me, for example, that we'll meet five hundred meters from my house, I can't picture the distance in my head. I get my bearings visually on a street by finding a store or some other place that I know. So I don't have much success in picturing the world. I do watch the international weather report on television and try to remember where places like Madrid, Paris, London, Beirut, and Tel Aviv are. I remember working near Tel Aviv with my father when I was still small, maybe about ten years old. We had been taken there to pick cauliflowers for a neighbor who had helped us harvest our wheat. There was a fence that protected us from the Jews because we were practically on their land. I thought you'd only have to cross over this fence to become Jewish, and that made me very afraid.

I have realized in adulthood that the memories that remain of my childhood are all linked to fear. For instance, I had been taught not to go near the Jews, because they were *halouf*, pigs. We were not even supposed to look at them so it was very bad for us to be there so close to them. We were taught that because they eat differently and live differently, they were not as good as us. We and they were like night and day, like wool and silk. That's what I was taught, that Jews are the wool and we Muslims are the silk. I don't even know why that was put in my head, but that was the only way of thinking. When you saw Jews in the street, and you almost never saw them anywhere else, fights would break out with stones and pieces of wood thrown. You were absolutely forbidden to go up to them or speak to them because if you did, you would become a Jew, too! But the Jewish people never did me any harm and I must realize once and for all that this is complete nonsense.

There is a very nice Jewish butcher shop in my current neighborhood and the meat there is better than I get elsewhere. But I don't dare go in alone to buy it myself because of this lingering fear. So I go to the Tunisian butcher just because he is Tunisian and not Jewish. Why, I don't know. I often tell myself: *Souad, you're going to go there and buy this fine meat, it's meat like any other.* I know I'll be able to do it one day but I'm still afraid. I heard too much at home that any contact with Jews was forbidden, that we had to ignore them as if they didn't exist on the same earth with us. It was more than hatred: They were the Muslims' worst enemy.

I was born Muslim, and while I am still Muslim and I believe in God, I retain a few of the customs of my village. I don't like war, I detest violence. If someone reproaches me for being critical of the Muslim religion by speaking badly of the men of my country—and this has happened—instead of arguing, I try to force the other person to listen to me by discussing the issue calmly. I want to help them understand what they haven't understood before. My mother frequently quarreled in anger with the neighbors. She would throw stones at them, or she would pull their hair. In our country, the women always go after the hair. I would hide behind the door, in the bread oven, or in the stable with the sheep because it was very upsetting and I didn't want to see it.

I would like to learn about everything I don't know, and come to a greater understanding of the differences in the world. It is my hope that my children will profit from the opportunities they have here. My own misfortune is actually responsible for their chances. It is destiny that has preserved them from the violence of my country, from the throwing of stones and the evil actions of men. I want them to have no part of all the wrong ideas that were put into my head and that I have so much difficulty getting rid of. I realize that

Burned Alive

if I had been told I had blue eyes and I had never seen myself in a mirror, all my life I would have believed I had blue eyes. The mirror represents culture, education, the knowledge of oneself and others. If I look at myself in a mirror, for example, I say to myself: *How small you are!* Without a mirror I wouldn't know this unless I walked next to a tall person.

I begin to realize that I know nothing about the Jews, or about their history, and that if I continue like this I, too, will convey the idea to my children that the Jew is a *halouf*. I will have passed on to them ignorance, instead of knowledge and the ability to learn to think for themselves.

Out of the blue one day, Antonio told Laetitia that he didn't want her ever to marry an Arab.

"Why, Papa? An Arab is like you, like any other person, like everybody."

I said to my husband: "It may be an Arab, a Jew, a Spaniard, an Italian. The most important thing is that they choose the person they love and that they are happy, because I haven't been."

I love Antonio but I don't know why he loves me and I have never had the courage to ask him, to say to him: *Look at me, where I come from and how I look. With all these scars, how is it that you want me when there are plenty of other women?*

It is strange all the same. When I'm talking to him on the telephone, I always ask the same question: "Where are you, sweetheart?" And when he tells me that he's at home, I am so relieved! I always have this fear of abandonment inside me, a fear that he doesn't love me anymore, that I'll be waiting alone in anguish, as I once waited for Marouan's father. I have dreamed several times that Antonio was with someone else. It was one more nightmare. This began two days after Nadia's birth. Antonio is with another

181

woman. They are walking arm in arm and I am saying to my daughter Laetitia: "Quick, go get Papa!" I don't dare go myself. My daughter is pulling on her father's coat and pleading, "No, Papa! Don't go with her! Come back!" She has to bring him back to me, and she is tugging at her father as hard as she can. There is no ending to this nightmare so I never know whether Antonio comes back. The last time, I woke up about three thirty in the morning and Antonio wasn't in bed. I got up to look for him and saw that he wasn't in his armchair and the television wasn't on. I rushed to the window to see if his car was there before realizing there was a light in his study and that he was working on his business accounts.

I want so much to be at peace, to have no more nightmares! But these emotions are always present: anguish, uncertainty, jealousy, permanent uneasiness about life. Something in me is broken but people often don't realize it because I always smile politely out of respect for others and to hide my anxieties. But when I see an attractive woman pass by, with beautiful hair, beautiful legs, and lovely skin, and when summer comes, a time for the swimming pool and light clothes . . .

My closet is full of clothes that button up to the neck. While I have bought other things to give myself pleasure, like low-cut dresses, or sleeveless blouses, I can only wear them under a jacket, which has to be buttoned to the neck. It is the same every summer. I am angry knowing that the pool opens May 6 and closes September 6. It drives me crazy and I want it to rain or turn chilly. I'm thinking only of myself, but despite myself. When it's too warm, I only go out early in the morning or late in the evening. I watch the weather reports and hear myself saying: "Well, good, it won't be nice tomorrow." And the children tell me that it's mean of me because they want to go to the pool.

If the temperature goes up to thirty degrees Celsius, I shut myself up in my room, lock the door, and cry. When I have the courage to go out wearing my two layers of clothes—that is, the one underneath that I'd like to be seen in, and the one on top that hides me—I'm afraid of the people I pass, wondering if they know about me and whether they wonder why I'm dressed for cold weather in the middle of summer. I love the autumn, the winter, and the spring. I'm lucky to be living in a country where there is strong sunlight only three or four months of the year. I was born in a year-round sunny climate but I could no longer live in one. I have all but forgotten that country and the long hours when the golden sun would scorch the earth, and how it turned a pale yellow in the gray sky before setting for the night. I don't want that kind of sun.

Sometimes when I look outside at the swimming pool, I hate it. It was built for the tenants' pleasure, of course, but for me it is anything but that. It was the pool that set off one dreadful depression. I was forty years old and it was the very beginning of the summer, a June that started off unusually warm. I had just come in from shopping, and I was looking out my window at some women who looked practically nude in their skimpy bathing suits. One of my neighbors, a very pretty girl, was just coming back from the pool in a bikini, a sarong over her shoulders, her bare-chested boyfriend at her side. I was alone in the apartment, obsessed by the idea that I couldn't do what they were doing. It seemed so unfair because it was so hot. So I went to my closet and spread out I don't know how many clothes on the bed before finding something reasonable, but I still didn't feel right. Short sleeves underneath, another shirt on top of that. It's too hot. Put on a lighter shirt that's too see-through but closed at the throat, I can't do it. A miniskirt, I can't do that because my legs were used for the skin grafts. Open neck, short sleeves, I can't do it because of the scars. Everything I laid out on the bed was *can't do it*. By then I was perspiring heavily and everything stuck to my skin.

I lay down on the bed and began to sob. I couldn't stand being closed up in this heat anymore while everyone else was outside with their skin exposed to the air. I could cry as much as I wanted because I was alone. The girls were still in school, which was across from the house. Eventually I looked at myself in the bedroom mirror and thought: *Look at yourself! Why are you alive? You can't go to the beach with your family. Even if you go, you'll keep them from staying in the water, they'll have to come home because of you. The girls are in school but when they come home they'll want to go to the pool. Happily for them they can, but not you! You can't even go to the swimming pool restaurant to have a coffee or drink a lemonade because you're afraid of being looked at. You're covered up from head to foot as though it were winter. People would think you're crazy! You're good for nothing! You're alive, but unable to live. You're just an object locked up in the house.*

Too many thoughts were colliding in my head. I went into the bathroom and took the bottle of sleeping pills that I had bought at the pharmacy, without a prescription, because I had trouble sleeping. I emptied the bottle and counted the pills. There were nineteen left and I swallowed them all. After a few minutes I felt very strange and everything was spinning. I opened the window, and I was crying as I looked out at Nadia and Laetitia's school, directly across from our building. I opened the apartment door, and I heard myself talking as if I were at the bottom of a well. My intention was to go up to the sixth floor to jump from the terrace. I was moving as if walking and talking in my sleep.

What will they become if I die? They love me. I put them into the world. Why? So they could suffer? It isn't enough to have suffered so much myself? I don't want them to suffer. We leave this life the three of us together or nothing. No, I can't do this because they need me. Antonio works. He says he's at work but maybe he's at the beach, I don't actually know where he is. But he knows very well where I am. I am at home because it is too hot and I can't go out. I can't dress the way I want. Why did this happen to me? What did I do to God? What did I do here on earth to deserve this?

I was in the hallway, crying and feeling very disoriented, but I went back into the apartment to close the window. Then I went into the hall, to the mailboxes, to wait for the girls. After that, I don't remember anything until the hospital. I had passed out because of the sleeping pills. They emptied my stomach and the doctor kept me under observation. The next day, I found myself in the psychiatric hospital. I saw a very nice woman psychiatrist. I wanted to smile politely when she came into the room, but I immediately burst into tears. She made me take a tranquilizer. Then she sat down beside me and asked me to tell her how it happened and why I took the pills and why I wanted to end my life. I explained about the sun, and the fire, the scars, the desire for death, and I began to cry again. I wasn't able to sort out what had gone on in my mind. The swimming pool, that stupid swimming pool had set it all in motion. Could it be that I had wanted to die because of a swimming pool?

"You know that this is the second time you've escaped death? First at the hands of your brother-in-law, and now you. I think that's a lot, and if you're not treated it could happen again. But I'm here to help you. Do you want that?"

The answer was yes, and I was in therapy with her for a month, and then she sent me to see another psychiatrist once a week on Wednesdays. It was the first time in my life since the fire that I had the chance to talk with someone who was there only to listen to me talk—about my parents, about my unhappiness, about Marouan . . . It wasn't easy for me. Sometimes I wanted to stop everything but I forced myself to continue because I knew that when I left the session I always felt good.

After a time, I found the psychiatrist too directive, as if she were telling me to take a right turn to get home when I knew I could only get there by going left. She was acting like a parent with a child. I was required to see her every Wednesday even though I wanted to go only when I felt like it or needed to. I would have preferred, too, that she ask me questions, talk to me, and look me in the eye instead of looking at the wall while she wrote her notes. For a year I resisted the temptation to run away, but I knew I wasn't being realistic. In wanting to die, I was denying the existence of my two daughters. I was thinking only of myself, wanting to get away without thinking of Antonio and our daughters.

Although I am better now, it is sometimes very painful. It can come over me at any time, but especially in summer. We are going to move far away from this swimming pool. However, even though our house will be at the edge of a road, summer will still come. Even in the mountains, or in the desert, it will be summer all the same.

Sometimes I feel that I would like not to get up in the morning, I would like to die and not suffer anymore. I have my family, friends around me, I make a real effort. But I'm ashamed of myself. If I had been burned or paralyzed in an accident, I would regard my scars differently. It would be fate; no one would be responsible, not even me. But my brother-in-law set fire to me, and it was the will of my father and my mother. It isn't destiny or fate that has made me as I am. What is the worst is that it deprived me of my skin, of my very self, not for a month or a year, but for my whole life.

And the terror comes back from time to time. Recently, we were watching a movie on television, a Western, two men were fighting in a stable. One of them, out of viciousness, lit a match and threw it into the hay, between the legs of his adversary, who caught fire and began to run in flames. I started to yell, I spit out what I was eating. I was like a crazy woman. Antonio said to me: "No, sweetheart, it's a movie, it's just a movie." And he turned off the television. He took me in his arms to calm me and repeated: "Honey, it's only the television. It's not real, it's a movie." I was all the way back there, I was running with flames over me. I didn't sleep that night. I have such a terror of fire that I freeze at the sight of the smallest flame. I watch Antonio when he lights a cigarette, I wait for the match to go out or the flame of the cigarette lighter to disappear. I don't watch television much because of this. I'm afraid of seeing again someone or something burning. My daughters are sensitive to my fears. As soon as they notice something that could shock me, they turn it off. I don't want them to light a match. Everything is electric in the house. I don't want to see fire in the kitchen or anywhere else. But one day, someone was playing with matches in front of me. He put some alcohol on a finger and he lit it. The skin didn't burn, it was a trick.

I stood up, overcome with both fright and anger: "You go do

that somewhere else! Me, I've been burned. You don't know what it's like!"

A fire in a fireplace doesn't frighten me, provided I don't go near it. Water doesn't bother me if it's lukewarm. But I'm afraid of everything that's hot. Fire, hot water, the oven, the burners on the stove, saucepans, electric coffeemakers that are always turned on, the television, which could catch fire, faulty electrical outlets, the vacuum cleaner, forgotten cigarettes . . . everything that can start a fire. My daughters are terrorized because of me. A fifteen-year-old girl who can't turn on an electric burner because of me, that's not normal. If I'm not there I don't want them to use the stove or boil water for pasta or tea. I have to be there, attentive, on edge, to be certain of turning everything off myself. There isn't a day that I go to bed without first checking the electric burners.

I live with this fear night and day. I know that I make life difficult for others, that my husband is patient but that he gets tired sometimes of a reasonless terror, that my daughters ought to be able to hold a saucepan without me trembling. They will have to do it one day.

Another fear came to me when I turned forty: the idea that Marouan had become a man, that I hadn't seen him in twenty years, that he knew that I was married and that he had sisters somewhere. But Laetitia and Nadia didn't know they had a brother. This lie weighed on me and I didn't speak of it to anyone. Antonio had known of Marouan's existence from the beginning, but we never spoke about it. Jacqueline continued her work; she would leave on missions and come back, sometimes successful, sometimes empty-handed. She knew but she respected my silence. She had asked me to participate in conferences to talk about the honor crime in front of other women. I owed it to myself to speak about my life as a burned woman, to bear witness as a survivor. I was practically the only one to do it after all these years.

And I continued to lie, not revealing Marouan's existence, persuading myself that I was still protecting my child from this horror. But he was almost a man. The big question was to know whether I was protecting Marouan, or if I was really just safeguarding my personal shame, my guilt in putting him up for adoption. It took me time to realize that it was all intertwined. In my village, there aren't any psychiatrists, the women don't ask themselves such questions. We are only guilty of being women.

My daughters have grown up, and the questions have become more hurtful.

"But why did they burn you, Mama?"

"Because I wanted to marry a boy I had chosen and because I was expecting a baby."

"What happened to the baby? Where is he?"

He stayed there in an orphanage. I couldn't tell them otherwise.

Surviving Witness

Jacqueline asked me to bear witness in the name of the SURGIR association. She waited until I was emotionally capable, after the depression that suddenly devastated me, even though I had succeeded in building a normal life. I was integrated into my new country, I was safe, with a husband and children. I was better, but I still felt fragile in front of these European women. I was going to speak to them about a world so different from their own, about cruelty so inexplicable for them.

I told my story in front of these women, sitting on a platform, before a small table with a microphone. Jacqueline was next to me. I threw myself into it from the start. And they asked me questions: "Why did he burn you? . . . What bad thing did you do? . . . He set fire to you just because you spoke to a man?" I never said I was expecting a child. I said that if they even gossip about you in the village, you can end up with the same punishment as someone who actually is pregnant. Jacqueline knows something about this. And especially, I said nothing about it to spare my son, who knew nothing of my past and his. I didn't give my real name; anonymity is a measure of safety. Jacqueline knows about cases where the family was able to find a daughter thousands of kilometers away and murder her.

A woman in the audience got up and asked: "Souad, your face is pretty, where are these scars?"

"Madame, I understand very well that you would ask me this question, I expected it. So I will show you where my scars are."

I got up, in front of everyone, and I undid my shirt. I was wearing a low-cut blouse and short sleeves underneath. I showed my arms, I showed my back. And this woman started to cry. The few men who were there were uncomfortable. They felt sorry for me. When I displayed myself in public I felt like a sort of sideshow freak. But it doesn't bother me so much doing it in this situation, in bearing witness, because this is important for people. I must make them understand that I am a survivor. I was dying when Jacqueline arrived in that hospital. I owe her my life, and the work she pursues with SURGIR requires a living witness to sensitize people to the honor crime. Most people don't know about it, quite simply because survivors are few in the world. And because, for their safety, they should not go public. They escaped the honor crime thanks to the shelters provided by this organization in several countries. It is in not only Jordan or the West Bank, but elsewhere in the Middle East, in India, in Pakistan. At this part of the program, Jacqueline takes over and explains that it is imperative to take safety measures for all these women.

At the time of my first testimony, I had been in Europe for about fifteen years. My life had completely changed. I can take risks that these other victims cannot take. The personal questions have to do with my new life but especially the condition of women in my country. A man asked me this question. I sometimes have difficulty expressing myself when it's a question of my own unhappy life. When it's about someone else, somehow I find the right words and take off.

"Sir, a woman there has no life. Many girls are beaten, mistreated, strangled, burned, killed. It's normal for us. My mother wanted to poison me to 'finish' my brother-in-law's work, and for her this was normal, it's part of her world. That's what a normal life is for us women there. You're beaten up, it's normal, you're burned, it's normal, you're mistreated, it's normal. The cow and the sheep, as my father used to say, are worth more than the women. If you don't want to die, you'd better keep quiet, obey, grovel, be a virgin when you're married, and bear sons. If I had not had an encounter with a man, that is the life I would have had. My children would have become like me, my grandchildren like my children. If I had lived there, I would have become 'normal' like my mother, who suffocated her own children. Maybe I would have killed my daughter. I could have let her burn to death. Now I think that it is monstrous! But if I had stayed there, I would have done the same! When I was in the hospital there, dying, I still thought all this was normal. But when I came to Europe, I began to understand, at the age of twenty-five, that there are countries where it is not acceptable to set a woman on fire, that girls are valued as much as boys. For me, the world stopped at my village. It was a wonderful place, it was the whole world, and it extended all the way to the market! Beyond the market, there were girls who wore makeup, who wore low-cut short dresses. They were the ones who weren't normal. My family was! We were pure as the sheep's wool, but the others, as soon as you got beyond the market, they were the impure ones!

"Girls couldn't go to school. Why? So they would know nothing of the rest of the world. We were controlled by our parents. Education, information, the law, what we know and believe comes to us only from our parents. What they say, we do. That's why there was no school for us. So we wouldn't take the bus, we wouldn't dress differently, wouldn't be holding a notebook in our hands, wouldn't be taught to read and write, that's being too intelligent, not good for a girl! My brother was the only son in the middle of girls, he dressed the way men do here, like in a big city, he went to the barber, to school, to the movies, he went out as he pleased, why? Because he had a penis between his legs! He was lucky, he had two boys, but in the end he's not the luckiest, it's his daughters. They have had the great fortune of not being born!

"The SURGIR Foundation, with Jacqueline, tries to save these girls. But it isn't easy. We're sitting here comfortably, I'm speaking to you and you're listening to me. But women in those other countries are suffering! It is for this reason that I bear witness for SURGIR about the honor crimes, because it continues! I am alive and I am on my feet thanks to the good God, thanks to Edmond Kaiser, and thanks to Jacqueline. SURGIR is a courageous organization and is working hard to help these girls. I admire the people of SURGIR. I don't know how they do it. I would rather bring food and clothing to refugees than do their work. You have to mistrust the world. You may speak to a woman who seems pleasant enough but who will denounce you because you want to help and she doesn't agree with you. When Jacqueline arrives in one of these countries, she is obliged to behave as they do, to eat, walk, and speak like them. She has to blend into that world, has to remain anonymous!"

"Thank you, Madame!"

In the beginning, I was in anguish, I didn't know how I was supposed to speak, and now Jacqueline had to tell me to stop talking! After a while, speaking in person before an audience didn't bother me too much. But I was afraid of the radio, because of the other people in my life, the people I work with, and especially my daughters, who knew some things about my other life but not everything. They were about eight and ten years old at the time, they had friends at school, I wanted to ask them to be discreet if they were asked questions. Laetitia thought it was great that Mama was going to be on the radio and wanted to come along. This was reassuring but at the same time a little disturbing. I realized that they didn't appreciate the significance of this witnessing and that apart from my scars, they knew almost nothing about my life. One day or another, when they would be bigger, I would have to tell them everything, and just thinking about it made me feel sick.

The radio interview was the first time that I was speaking to such a large audience. My daughters learned a new piece of my story from this broadcast. After listening to the program, Laetitia had a very violent reaction.

"You get dressed now, Mama, you get your suitcase, we're going to take a plane and go to your village. We're going to do the same thing to them. We're going to burn them! We're going to take some matches and we're going to burn them just the way they did it to you! I can't stand to see you like this."

She was treated by a psychologist for six months but one day she said she didn't want to go back, that I was as good for her as the psychologist because she could talk to me about everything. I didn't want to force her. I telephoned the doctor and we settled the bill. He thought that she needed a few supplemental sessions but for the time being she should not be forced. "But if you see later that she isn't well, that she doesn't speak readily, that she is depressed, I would like you to bring her back."

I fear my history weighs heavily on them, now and into their future. They're afraid for me, and I'm afraid for them. I waited until they were mature enough to understand everything else that I had not yet said: my life before in detail, the man I wanted for a husband, Marouan's father. I fear this revelation, much more than all the testimony they can ask of me. I must also help Laetitia and Nadia not to hate the country I come from, and which is half theirs. They are in total ignorance of what goes on there. How can I keep them from hating the men of this country? The land there is beautiful, but the men are bad. In the West Bank, there are women who fight for legal protection. But it is the men who vote the laws.

At this very moment there are women in prison in certain countries. They are there because it is the only means of sheltering them and preventing their death. Even in prison they are not completely safe. But the men who want to kill them, they are at liberty. The law doesn't punish them, or so little that their hands are soon free again to slit throats, burn, avenge their so-called honor. If someone came forward in a village, in a neighborhood, to stop the avengers from doing harm, there would be ten others coming after the protester, a hundred up against the ten who object. If a judge treated an honor crime as a murder and sentenced a man accordingly, that judge could never again walk down the street, he could not continue living in the village, he would have to flee in shame for having punished a "hero."

I wonder what became of my brother-in-law. Did he go to prison for a few days? My mother spoke of the police, the troubles my brother and brother-in-law could have if I didn't die. Why didn't the police come to see me? I was the victim, with third-degree burns!

I have met girls who have come from afar, as I did years ago. They are in hiding. A young girl who has no legs: She was attacked by two neighbor men who tied her up and put her in the path of a train. Another whose father and brother tried to murder by stabbing her and throwing her into a garbage bin. Still another whose mother and two brothers threw her out a window: She is paralyzed. And the others no one talks about, the ones who have been found too late, dead. And the ones who succeeded in fleeing but were caught in another country and killed. And those who have been able to escape in time and go into hiding, with or without a child, virgins or mothers.

I have never met any burned women like myself; they haven't survived. And still I hide, I cannot say my real name, show my face. I can only speak out, it is the only weapon I have.

Jacqueline

My role today and in the years to come is to continue working to save other Souads. It will be a long struggle, complicated and arduous, and money is needed, as always. Our foundation is called SURGIR, which means "arise," because the right moment must "arise" to help these women escape death. We work no matter where the need is in the world—for example, in Afghanistan, Morocco, Chad—anywhere there is an urgent need for intervention. The larger world has been, and continues to be, very slow to respond to the atrocities that are inflicted on women in this part of the world. It has been reported that more than six thousand honor crimes are committed in a year, and behind this figure are all the suicides and "accidents" that cannot be counted.

In some countries, women are put in prison when they have the courage to complain, supposedly to save their lives. Some have been there for fifteen years because the only people who can get them out of there are the father or the brother, which is to say the very ones who want to kill them. So if a father asks for his daughter to be released, it is quite evident that the warden is not going to comply! I am aware of one or two women who were released, and they were subsequently killed.

In Jordan, and this is only one example, there is a law on the books, as there is in most countries, that a murder must be punished by years in prison. But next to this law, are two small articles, ninety-seven and ninety-eight, specifying that judges will be lenient with those found guilty of honor crimes. The penalty is generally six months to two years in prison. The condemned, sometimes considered heroes, usually do not serve the whole sentence. Associations of local female attorneys are struggling to have these articles amended. Some other articles have been changed, but not ninety-seven and ninety-eight.

We work on-site with associates of women that, for several years now, have initiated programs for preventing violence toward women and for assisting women who are victims of violence in their countries. Their work is long and often thwarted by obstacles. But step by step things have moved forward. The women of Iran have made progress on the issue of their civil rights. Women of the Middle East have learned that there are laws in their countries that concern them and give them rights. Appeals have been submitted to the parliaments, and certain articles of law have been amended.

Little by little, the authorities recognize these crimes. Statistics are published officially in the reports of the Human Rights Commission in Pakistan. In the Middle East, public health law provides information on the number of known cases, and local associations inquire into cases of violence and do research into the historical and current reasons for maintaining these archaic customs. Whether it is in Pakistan, which keeps track of the number of girls and women killed, in the Middle East, or in Turkey, the most important work is to put an end to these customs, which are blindly passed on. In recent years, authorities such as King Hussein and Prince Hassan have come out openly against honor crimes, which they have said "are not crimes of honor but of dishonor." Imams and religious Christians explain continually that the honor crime is totally foreign to the Koran and the Bible.

We do not lose courage or our determination. SURGIR has developed the habit of knocking on all doors, risking having them slam in our faces. Sometimes it works.

My Son

Laetitia and Nadia were still small when I returned for a visit to my adoptive parents for the first time since I had left Marouan with them. I feared Marouan's reaction face to face with his two little sisters. He was becoming an adolescent, I had built another life without him, and I didn't know if he was going to remember me, if he would hold it against me or have no interest in us. Every time I telephoned to alert them of my visit and my uneasiness, they would tell me: "No, no, no problem, Marouan knows about it, you can come."

But he wasn't there very often. I asked about him and they assured me that he was doing fine. I had seen him three times in twenty years. And I was unhappy every time. I would cry when I went home. My two daughters encountered their brother without knowing who he was, while he knew everything. He showed nothing, demanded nothing, and I kept silent. The visits were exhausting. I couldn't speak to him because I didn't have the strength.

The last time, Antonio said to me: "I think it's better if you don't go there anymore. You cry all the time, you become depressed and it doesn't serve any purpose. He has his life, parents, a family, friends . . . let him be. Someday later on, you can explain it all to him if he asks."

I always felt guilty, I refused to go back to the past, so much more so because no one knew I had a son, except for Jacqueline and my husband. Was he still my son? I didn't want any family crisis, it would be much too difficult.

The last time I had seen Marouan, he had been about fifteen years old. He even played a little with his sisters. Our exchange was limited to a few words of sad banality: "Hello, how are things?" "Fine and you?"

Almost ten years passed. I thought he had forgotten me, that I no longer existed in his life now that he was an adult man. I knew that he was working and that he was living in a small apartment with a girlfriend, like all the young people his age.

Laetitia was thirteen and Nadia twelve. I devoted myself to their education and persuaded myself that I had done my duty. In the moments of depression, for my own sake, I would say to myself that in order to continue to survive it was better to forget. I envied happy people, those who have had no unhappiness in their childhood, who have no secret, no double life. I wanted to bury my first life and, with all my strength, to try to be like the happy people. But every time that I took part in a conference when I had to tell about this nightmare life, my happiness trembled on its base, like a badly built house. Antonio saw it clearly, and Jacqueline, too. I was fragile, but I pretended not to be.

One day, Jacqueline said to me: "You know, you could do a real service to other women if you would make a book of your life."

"A book? But I hardly know how to write . . ."

"But you can speak."

I didn't now that you could "speak" a book. A book is something so important. I'm not one of those who read books, unfortunately. My daughters read books, Antonio can read them. I prefer the morning paper. I was so impressed by the idea of a book, of myself in a book, that I couldn't get it out of my head. Seeing my daughters get bigger, I said to myself that one day I would have to tell them more. If it was all written in a book once and for all, it would be less agonizing than facing my daughters alone. Until now, I had only told them the essential details to explain my physical appearance. But one day or another, they would want to know everything, and the questions that would come would be so many knife thrusts to my heart.

I didn't feel capable of rummaging in my memory searching for the details of the past. By force of wanting so desperately to forget, you really do forget. The psychiatrist had explained to me that this was normal, a result of the shock and the suffering due to the lack of care. But the gravest issue was Marouan. I had been living for so long under a protective lie. And I had been doing it badly.

If I agreed to tell about myself in a book, I would have to talk about Marouan. Did I have the right to do this? I said no. I was too afraid. My safety and his were equally at stake. A book goes everywhere in the world. And what if my family were to find me? If they were to harm Marouan? They were capable of it, for sure. On the other hand, I wanted to do it. Too often I had daydreamed about an impossible vengeance. I saw myself returning there, well concealed and protected until I found my brother. It was like a film in my head. I arrive at his house and I say: *Do you remember me, Assad? You see, I am alive. Take a good look at my scars. It was your brother-in-law Hussein who burned me, but here I am!*

Do you remember my sister Hanan? What did you do with my sister? Did you give her to the dogs? And your wife, how is she? Why was I burned on the day she gave birth to your sons? I was pregnant, did you have to burn my son, too? Explain to me why you did nothing to help me, you, my only brother.

I introduce my son, Marouan! He was born two months prematurely in the city hospital, but he is big and handsome, and full of life! Look at him!

And Hussein? Has he grown old or is he dead? I hope he's still here, but maimed or paralyzed, to see me alive in front of him! I hope he is suffering as much as I suffered!

And my father and mother? Are they dead? Tell me where they are so I can go and curse their graves.

I often have this dream of vengeance. It makes me violent, like them, and I want to kill like them! They all believe I'm dead, and I would so much like for them to see me alive!

For almost a year, I said no to the book unless I could leave my son out of the story. Jacqueline respected my decision. She thought it was too bad, but she understood.

I did not want to do a book about myself without talking about him, and I couldn't decide whether to have a face-to-face meeting with Marouan to resolve the problem. Life went on but I was demoralized from saying to myself: *Do it! No, don't do it!* But how to approach Marouan? I considered the idea that one day I would telephone him, just like that without warning after all these years, and say to him: *Marouan, we have to talk.*

How should I introduce myself? Mama? How should I act in

front of him? Hug him? And if he's forgotten me? He has a right to, since I more or less forgot him myself.

And Jacqueline forced me to reflect on something that tormented me even more. "What would happen if Marouan one day met one of his sisters and she didn't know that he is her brother? If she fell in love with him and brought him home, what would you do?"

I had never thought about that possibility. About twenty kilometers separated us. Laetitia was going to be fourteen and pretty soon the time for boyfriends would arrive. Nadia would follow. Twenty kilometers is nothing. The world is small. Despite this awful possibility I still couldn't make up my mind. Another year went by. And finally things sorted themselves out. Marouan telephoned. I was at work and it was Nadia who answered. He simply said: "I know your mother, we were together in the same foster family. Can you ask her to call me back?"

But when I came home, Nadia couldn't find the piece of paper on which she'd written the number! She looked everywhere. I was a nervous wreck. You might have thought that fate didn't want me to be in contact with Marouan. I didn't know where he was living or where he worked now. I could have telephoned his adoptive father to get the information but I didn't have the courage. I was cowardly and I hated myself for it. It was easier to let fate take its course than to look at myself in the mirror. He called back on Thursday. He was the one who said: "We need to speak with each other," and we arranged to meet the next day at noon. I was going to face my son, and I dreaded what I knew was waiting for me. In short, the questions would be, *Why was I adopted when I was five years old? Why didn't you keep me with you? Please explain it to me.*

I wanted to look nice so I had my hair done, put on makeup, dressed simply in jeans and a red blouse with long sleeves and closed neck. The meeting was fixed for exactly noon, in front of a restaurant in the city.

The street is narrow. He comes from the downtown area and I from the railroad station so we can't miss each other. I knew I would recognize him among thousands. I see him coming from a distance, carrying a green sports bag. In my mind he was still an adolescent but this is a man who is smiling at me. My legs won't hold me, my hands begin to tremble, and my heart pounds as if I am meeting the man in my life. It is a love encounter. He is tall so he has to bend down to kiss me, very simply, as if he'd left me the day before, and I return his kiss.

"You did right to call," I say.

"I also called two weeks ago and since you didn't call back, I thought: *So, there it is, she doesn't want to see me.*"

I told him that Nadia had lost the number.

"If I hadn't called again yesterday, would you have called me?" he asks.

"I don't know, I don't think so, no. I didn't dare because of your parents. I know that Mama died . . ."

"Yes, Papa is all alone now, but it's okay. And you?"

He doesn't know what to call me. This habit that I developed in the beginning of calling the foster parents "Papa" and "Mama" doesn't help things. Who is his mama?

I plunge ahead: "You know, Marouan, you can call me Mama, you can call me Souad, you can call me the little one, the big one, you can call me whatever you like. And if God is willing, we'll get to know each other quickly."

"Agreed. Let's have lunch and talk."

We sit down at a table, and I devour him with my eyes. He resembles his father. Same silhouette, same fast gait, same expression, but he is different. Also, he looks a little like my brother but with calm, softer features. He appears to take life as it comes, without too much complication. He is simple and direct.

"Explain to me how you were burned."

"Do you mean that you don't know, Marouan?"

"No. No one has ever told me anything."

I explain and, as I speak, I see his expression change. When I talk about the flames covering my body, he puts down the cigarette he was going to light.

"I was inside you?"

"Yes, you were in my belly. I gave birth all alone. I didn't feel your arrival because of my burns. I saw you, you were between my legs, that's all. Afterward you disappeared. They took you away from me. They put me in a hospital to die. Then Jacqueline searched for you so she could take us out of the country together by plane. We lived together for nine months in a shelter and then we were placed with Papa and Mama."

"So it's because of me, your burns?"

"No, it's not because of you! No, never! It's unfortunately the custom of our country. The men in this country make their own law. The ones to blame are my parents, my brother-in-law, but surely not you!"

He looks at my scars, my ears, my neck, and then places his hand gently on my arm. I know that he guesses the rest, but he doesn't ask to see. Is he afraid to ask?

"You don't want to see . . ."

"No. This story already breaks my heart, it would give me more pain. What was my father like? Did he look like me?"

"Yes, the upper part of your face. I haven't seen you walk much, but you hold yourself like him, straight, proud. And the back of your neck, your mouth, and especially your hands, even the nails. He was a little taller, muscular like you. He was handsome. Earlier when I looked at your shoulders I thought I was seeing your father."

"That must warm your heart, because you must have loved him."

"Oh yes, of course I loved him. He had promised that we would get married, but you see, when he learned that I was pregnant, he didn't come back."

"That's disgusting! To drop you! So, in the end, it is because of me."

"Marouan, no. Never think that. It's because of the men there. Later, when you get to know that culture better, you will understand."

"I'd really like to meet him one day. Couldn't we go there? The two of us, just to see what it's like, and then see him. It would please me to see his face. Does he know that I exist?"

"That would surprise me. I never saw him again. And then there is the war there. No, it's better for both of us not to ever see them again."

"Is it true that you gave birth at seven months?"

"Yes, that's true. I was all alone when you arrived, I didn't get to see you for very long, but you were very small."

"What time did it happen?"

"The time? I don't know. It was October first they told me later. The important thing is that you were whole, from head to foot!"

"Why didn't you speak to me when you used to come to visit Mama and Papa?"

"I didn't dare in front of Papa and Mama who had adopted you. I didn't want to hurt them. They are the ones who raised you, and they did everything they could for you."

"I remember you. And in the bedroom once, you gave me a yogurt and then one of my teeth fell out and there was blood in the yogurt and I didn't want to eat it but you made me eat it. I remember that."

"I don't remember. You know at the time I was taking care of other children and Mama would tell me that I shouldn't spend more time with you than with the others . . . And also we didn't waste food in their house because it was very expensive to care for all the children."

"When I was fourteen or fifteen, I was really mad at you, you know . . . I was jealous."

"Jealous of who?" I ask.

"Jealous of you," he says. "I wanted to be with you all the time."

"And now? Today?"

"I want to get to know you, I want to know so many things."

"You don't hold it against me for having other children?"

"It's great to have sisters and I'd like to get to know them, too."

He looked at his watch. It was also time for me to go back to work.

"It's too bad you have to leave," says Marouan. "I'd like to stay here with you."

"Yes, but I have to. Can you come to the house tomorrow?"

"No," he says. "It's too soon. I prefer we see each other again somewhere else."

"So tomorrow evening, at seven o'clock, same place. I'll come with the girls."

He seemed very happy. I didn't expect it to be so easy because I believed he would so much hold it against me for having him adopted, that he would despise me. But he didn't even ask the question. He hugs me, I hug him back, and we say, "Good-bye and see you tomorrow."

And I get back to work, my head is buzzing like a beehive. An enormous weight is behind me.

Whatever happened now, I am rid of an anguish that was eating at me for so long, and that I couldn't admit. I regret not having been capable of keeping my son with me. One day I must ask him truly to forgive me for having left him behind in my efforts to remake my life. I couldn't really think straight at the time. I didn't know what I was doing. Nothing was real. I was floating. I should have told him that and also that even if his father abandoned both of us, I loved him, this man. It wasn't my fault if he was a coward like the others. I should tell him also: *Marouan, I was so afraid that I beat on my stomach in an attempt to abort.* He must forgive me for doing that. I thought that the blood would come to deliver me, I was too ignorant and I was terrified. Will he be able to understand and forgive me? Can I tell everything to this son? And to my daughters? How are all three of them going to judge me?

I was so overwhelmed that I didn't sleep that night. Once again, I see the flames on me and I run in the garden like a madwoman.

Antonio lets me work it out alone and he doesn't want to get involved for the time being. But he can see very well how bad off I am.

"Did you speak to the girls?"

"Not yet. Tomorrow. We're going to have dinner together with Marouan, and I'll find the right moment to speak to them. But I'm afraid, Antonio."

"You'll do it. There's no going back now."

At three fifty-seven in the morning, I found a message from Marouan on my portable phone: "It's just to tell you that I'm fine. I send you a kiss. Until tomorrow, Mama."

He made me cry.

To Build a House

That evening, Antonio went out with a friend to leave me alone with the girls. It is Saturday evening, seven o'clock, November 16, 2002. The dinner is lively. They devour everything. They laugh at everything. Laetitia is very talkative, chattering as usual. Marouan brought his girlfriend. To my girls, he is still officially only one of the children that I knew in my foster family. His presence doesn't surprise them and they are happy to go out on a Saturday evening with Mama and pals.

They didn't grow up together and yet they seem to be so compatible. I had been fearing that this little gathering would be trying. Antonio was concerned and said before he left: "Call me if you need me and I'll come get you."

It's strange but I feel fine and I have almost no more fear, only a little uneasiness for my two daughters. Marouan teases the older one. "Come on, Laetitia, sit next to me." He pulls her close to him and jokes.

And she turns to me and whispers: "He's so nice, Mama! And he's so good looking!"

"Yes, he is."

I observe the details of their three faces. Marouan resembles Laetitia somewhat, the top of the forehead perhaps. Now and then I also see in him an expression belonging to Nadia, more pensive and reserved than her sister. Laetitia always expresses her feelings, and her reactions are sometimes too impulsive. She inherited the Italian side from her father. Nadia keeps her thoughts and feelings more to herself.

Are they going to understand? My tendency is to see them as little three-year-old kids and to be overprotective. At Laetitia's age, my mother was already married and pregnant.

She has just said to me: "How good looking he is . . ." She might fall in love with her brother! My silence might have unleashed a series of catastrophes. For the moment they burst out laughing, making fun of a man who is quite drunk. He looks at our table, and yells over to Marouan: "You're lucky to be with women! Four women and I'm all alone!"

Marouan is proud and takes offense. He mutters: "I'm going to go over there and smash his face!"

"No, stay where you are, please!"

"All right."

The owner of the restaurant takes care of moving the intruder away quietly and the meal ends in pleasantries and laughter.

We are going to accompany Marouan and his friend to the railroad station. He lives and works in the country. My son takes care of gardens and the maintenance of parks. He seems to like his work and he talked about it a little at the table. Laetitia and Nadia don't yet have clear plans at their age. Nadia talks about working in fashion design; Laetitia goes from one idea to another. All three of them walk in front of me in the street that leads to the railroad station. Marouan is in the middle and Laetitia holds one of his arms, Nadia the other. It's the first time in their lives that they've done that, and they do it confidently. I still haven't said anything, and Marouan is wonderful. He just lets things go along. He whispers with his two sisters so naturally, as if he'd always known them. I didn't have much joy in my life before my marriage to Antonio and the birth of my two girls. Marouan was born in suffering, without a father, and they were born in happiness and are their father's treasures. Their destinies are different, but their laughter unites them better than I possibly could. New feelings come over me. I am proud of them. This evening I lack for nothing. No more anguish or sadness, only peace in my mind.

On the platform in the station, Laetitia says to me: "I've never felt as comfortable with anyone as with Marouan."

And Nadia adds: "Me, too . . ."

"I would like to go spend the night at Marouan's with his girlfriend, and then tomorrow we could have lunch together, and then take the train to come back!"

"No, we have to go home, Laetitia, your father's waiting for us."

"He's just so nice, Mama, I really like him. He's nice, he's handsome . . . Is he ever handsome, Mama!"

It's Nadia's turn to hang on me: "When will we see him again, Mama?"

"Perhaps tomorrow or the next day. Mama will arrange things, you'll see."

"What's she saying, Nadia?"

"I asked Mama if we could see Marouan again and she said okay for tomorrow, no, Mama? It's okay?"

"You can count on me. Mama will do it . . ."

The train leaves, I look at the station clock and see that it's one forty-eight in the morning. They both run, sending kisses with their hands. I'll never forget that moment. Since I've lived in Europe, I've become used to watches, and this habit has become almost an obsession. My memory of the past fails me so often that I conscientiously note the present when it's important for me. It's funny, Marouan wanted to know yesterday what time he was born. He needs anchoring, too. The details of my past are a gift I would have trouble giving him. Everything that I could pull out of my poor head, I thought about that night, in my insomnia. I thought I had seen an electric light in the corridor of that wretched hospital when a doctor took my son away. The precise time? That is a Western concept. In our land only the men have a watch. For twenty years, I had to content myself with only the sun and the moon. I will tell Marouan that he was born at the hour of the moon.

I leave a message on his cell phone when we get home, to check if they've gotten home all right. He answers with a "thank you, good night, see you tomorrow."

It is late and the girls go right to bed. Antonio isn't asleep yet. "How did it go, sweetheart?"

"Perfect."

"Have you talked to the girls?"

"No, not yet. But I'm ready to tell them tomorrow. I don't have a reason anymore for waiting. They liked him immediately. It's strange but it is as if they'd known him for a long time."

"Marouan didn't say anything, he didn't make reference to anything?"

"Absolutely nothing, he was terrific. But it's strange that Laetitia became attached to him like that, and Nadia, too. They were hanging on him. They never behave that way with their friends. Never . . ."

"Are you nervous?"

I'm not nervous, I'm curious. Can brothers and sisters recognize each other this way? What happens between them for it to become so evident to them that they are somehow connected? Is there a signal, something they have in common without even knowing it? I was expecting anything and nothing at the same time, but not this instinctive affection.

"Maybe you ought to wait a day or two."

"No. Tomorrow is Sunday, I'll go to the office cafeteria because there won't be anyone there, and I'll speak to Laetitia and Nadia calmly. We'll see what God gives us, Antonio."

After my daughters, there will be the others I must tell, the neighbors, and especially the office where I've worked for some years. My job is to organize small receptions. I am at home there, and the friendship of my bosses means a lot to me. How to introduce Marouan to them as my son after ten years?

I need to be alone with my daughters. They are going to judge their mother on a lie of twenty years, and may also see me now as a woman they don't know, as Marouan's mother, who hid him all these years. The mother who loves them and protects them. I have often told them that their birth is the great happiness of my life. How will they be able to understand that Marouan's birth was such a nightmare and why I never said anything?

The next morning, Sunday, I woke up as usual about nine o'clock. Laetitia asked if I wanted her to make me a coffee. It's the morning ritual and I always answer, "Yes, please." I am stubborn about politeness and mutual respect. I find the children here are sometimes badly raised. The language that they hear at school is vulgar, and Antonio and I firmly object to it. Laetitia's been scolded more than once by her father for a sassy response. I only had the education of a slave.

Laetitia brings me coffee and a glass of warm water. She hugs me casually and Nadia, too. The love that I receive from them and their father surprises me every day, and I wonder how I deserve it. What I'm about to do is as hard for other reasons as was my fear of facing my son.

"I would like to speak to you about something very important."

"Okay, Mama, we're listening."

I tell them that we will go to the office cafeteria to talk.

"But you're not working today! You know, I was thinking again about last night. It was too super! Has Marouan called you yet?"

"We stayed out late. He must still be sleeping."

If he weren't her brother, I'd be worried. They talk between themselves, absolutely not concerned about this unusual trip to the office on a Sunday morning. I'm the one who's nervous. They're going out with Mama, who is going to the office to do something, and then . . . It doesn't matter, they trust me.

"Last evening, we had a wonderful time. Is that what you wanted to talk to us about?"

"Wait, first things first . . . So, last night we had a wonderful time with Marouan. Doesn't that say anything to you? Marouan? That makes you think about what?"

"About a nice boy who lived with your adoptive parents, he said so . . . And he's so good looking and he's so nice."

"Is it his attractiveness or the fact that he's nice that attracts you to him?"

"Everything, Mama. He just seems very gentle."

"That's true. Do you remember that I was pregnant when I was burned? I talked to you about that."

"Yes, you told us . . ."

"But where do you think that child is?"

They look into my eyes, strangely.

"But he stayed there! In your family!"

"No. You have no idea where this child might be? You've never seen anyone who resembles you, Laetitia, or you, Nadia? Or even me, someone who might have the same voice, who might walk like me?"

"No, Mama. I promise, no."

"No, Mama."

Nadia is satisfied with repeating what her sister says. Laetitia is usually the spokesperson, but yesterday I saw a little trace of jealousy appear in Nadia. Marouan was laughing more with Laetitia, and he paid a little less attention to Nadia. She listens to me very attentively now and doesn't take her eyes off me.

"You, either, Nadia, you don't know?"

"No, Mama."

"Laetitia, you're older, you could remember? You certainly saw him at my adoptive parents' house."

"Honest, Mama. No."

"All right then, it's Marouan!"

"Ah, my God, it's Marouan, who we were with last night!"

And they both burst into tears.

"He's our brother, Mama! He was in your stomach!"

"He's your brother, he was in my stomach, and I gave birth to him all alone. But I didn't leave him there, he was here with me."

Now comes the most difficult explanation, the reason for the adoption. I pick my words carefully, words that I had already heard from the psychiatrist, *build a new life, self-acceptance, become a woman again, become a mother again . . .*

"You kept this inside yourself for twenty years, Mama! Why didn't you tell us sooner?"

"You were much too young and I didn't know how you were going to react. I wanted to tell you when you were older. The same is true about how I got the scars . . . and the fire. It's like building a house: You have to put one brick after the other. If one brick isn't solid, what will happen? The other bricks fall. So it's the same thing with this, my sweethearts. Mama wanted to rebuild her house and I thought that later it would be more solid and tall enough to allow Marouan to enter it. If not, it could collapse, my house, and I wouldn't have been able to do anything. But now he's here. It's for you to choose what's next."

"He's our brother, Mama. Tell him to come live with us. How about it, Nadia? We have a big brother and I've dreamed of having a big brother, and I always said so, a big brother like my girlfriends have. And now I have a big brother, he's here, it's Marouan! Right, Nadia?"

"I'll clean out my closet and I'll even give him my bed!"

Now, Nadia wouldn't give me a piece of chewing gum! She is very generous but doesn't easily give away her things. But for her brother, she'd do it! It's amazing, this brother who pops up out of nowhere, and here she is ready to give him everything! So that is how the unknown big brother came into the house. As simple as emptying a closet and giving him her bed. Soon we'll have a bigger house, there will be a room for him. I am consumed with happiness. They spend a lot of time calling each other on the telephone, waiting for each other, and I tell myself it won't take long for them to squabble. But Marouan is the big brother and he immediately assumes authority with his sisters: "Laetitia, you don't answer your mother in that tone! She asked you to turn down the television, and you should do it! You're lucky to have your parents, you must respect them!"

"Okay, okay, I'm sorry, I'll be better, promise . . ."

"I didn't come here for us to quarrel, but Papa and Mama both work. So what about this messy room?"

"But we work hard at school, too. You've done it and you know how hard it is!"

"Yes, true, but that's no reason to treat Papa and Mama like that."

And then Marouan took me aside: "Mama, what does Antonio think? Does it bother him if I take on the girls?"

"Antonio is happy with what you do."

"I'm afraid he'll tell me someday to mind my own business, these are his daughters."

But Antonio didn't do that. It was intelligent of him. On the contrary, he's very pleased to delegate a little of his authority. And the best is that they obey their brother better than they do their father or mother. With us they argue, they're capable of slamming a door, but not with him. I hold my breath and hope it lasts. Sometimes it's a little strained. Laetitia comes into my bed for refuge and then tells me Marouan gets on her nerves.

So I tell her: "He's right, the way your father's right. You do talk back."

"Why does he say he'll go away if we don't listen to him? And that he didn't come here to have to bawl us out?"

"That's normal. Marouan didn't have your good fortune, he's been through difficult times that you can't understand. Parents are important for him, a mother is precious when you haven't had her with you, you know?"

If I could only get rid of this guilt that still resurfaces all too often. If I could change my skin. I told Marouan that I had decided to put our story into a book, if he agreed.

"It will be like our family album. And a witness against the honor crime."

"One day, I'll go there," Marouan says.

"What will you go there for, Marouan? Vengeance? Blood? You were born there but you don't know what the men there are like. I dream about it, too. I feel hatred, too. I think it would soothe me to arrive in my village with you and shout at them: *Look everybody! This is Marouan, my son! We were burned, but we aren't dead! Look how handsome and strong and intelligent he is!*"

"It's my father I would like to see close up!" Marouan says. "I would like to understand why he dropped you, especially when he knew what was waiting for you."

"Perhaps. But you will understand better when it is in a book. I will tell everything that you still don't know, and what many people don't know about. Because there aren't many survivors, and the women who have survived still hide and for many years. They have lived in fear and they go on living in fear. I can bear witness for them."

He asked me if I was afraid, and I admitted I was a little. I'm especially afraid that my children, and Marouan in particular, will live with the thorn of vengeance; that this vengeance, which is passed along between generations, will leave a mark, even a very small one, in their minds. Marouan, too, must build a house, brick by brick. A book is a good thing for building a house.

I received a letter from my son, written in a nice round hand. He wanted to encourage me to undertake this difficult work. It made me cry one more time:

Mama,

After all this time of living alone, without you, to finally see you again, in spite of everything that has happened, has given me hope for a new life. I think of you and your courage. Thank you for making this book for us. It will bring me, too, courage in life. I love you, Mama.

Your son,

Marouan

I have told the story of my life for the first time by forcing out of my memory the things that were buried the deepest. It was more challenging than a public testimony, and more painful than answering the children's questions. I hope that this book will travel in the world, that it will reach the West Bank, and that the men will not burn it.

In our house, it will be displayed in a bookcase. And everything will have been said once and for all. I will have it bound in a pretty leather so that it isn't damaged, and with beautiful gold lettering.

Thank you.

Souad
Somewhere in Europe
December 31, 2002

Afterword

SURGIR is a Swiss foundation that works with women, anywhere in the world, who are subjected to criminal traditions, women who are martyrs in their souls and in their bodies, and with the children of these women. SURGIR fights vigorously against the injustice of the customs that victimize these women.

To support the work of SURGIR:

Banque Cantonale Vaudoise
1001 Lausanne
Account number: U 5060.57.74
To learn more about SURGIR: www.surgir.ch
Contact: office@surgir.ch